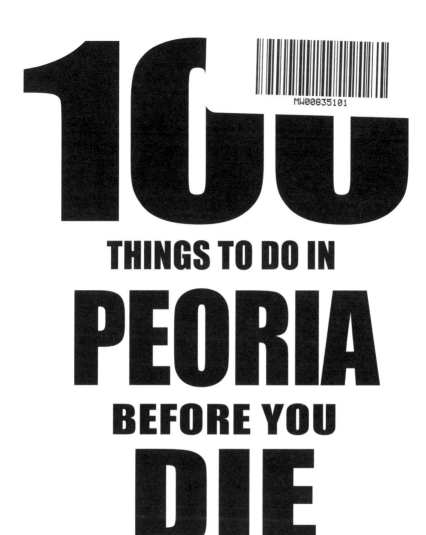

100

THINGS TO DO IN

PEORIA

BEFORE YOU

DIE

100

THINGS TO DO IN

PEORIA

BEFORE YOU

DIE

MOLLY CRUSEN BISHOP

REEDY PRESS

Library of Congress Control Number: 2022936988

ISBN: 9781681063911

Design by Jill Halpin

All images were provided by the author unless otherwise noted.
On the cover: Murray Baker Bridge, courtesty of Nicholas Windsor II

Printed in the United States of America
22 23 24 25 26   5 4 3 2 1

DEDICATION

For my parents, Don and Joani Crusen, who inspired a zest for life, and blooming where you are planted.

For my husband, Douglas Bishop, who has helped me build a foundation of love, family, adventure, and supports me in all of my endeavors.

For my children and grandchildren, Amanda, Brennan, Maggie, Grant, Jack, Tadd, Bella, Thea, and Dominic, may you always find adventures.

For Peoria, the city that holds my heart and soul forever.

• •

CONTENTS

Music and Entertainment

• •

• •

Sports and Recreation

● ●

Culture and History

PREFACE

Growing up on Peoria's historic West Bluff, in the humble but lovely house built in the 1880s by my great-grandparents, Patrick and Ellen McGowan Needham, planted the deep roots of love I have for this wonderful city. Many souls and stories began in that modest home they built. Patrick and Ellen were born in County Leitrim, Ireland, and courageously left their homeland in pursuit of the American dream. Their travels took them to Liverpool, Brooklyn, and St. Louis, and they finally settled in Peoria, Illinois, in the 1870s, making it their home forever. There have been more than five generations that followed, who have lived, loved, and helped build part of Peoria's story. Patrick and Ellen's son Charlie, my grandfather, was a writer who chronicled parts of his childhood in the late 1800s. My ancestors passed me the torch to continue being a story-keeper of this amazing city, and it is truly an honor to share *100 Things to Do in Peoria Before You Die*.

As a young girl, I never imagined living my entire life in Peoria, but as love and family often do, with a growing family of my own, I was firmly planted in Peoria, and have definitely bloomed where I was planted. As a local historian, writer, and speaker, my research on Peoria's past established a fervent intrigue, not only on what built Peoria but also on what is making her tick today! Peoria's history is deep and rich; its community is lovely and vibrant. My original list for this book was over 300 things to do, and it was really not hard to gather. I could have gone on for many more hundreds of things.

• •

Peoria, Illinois, is smack-dab in the middle of the Midwest. Pretty much halfway between St. Louis and Chicago, it is a proud metropolitan city with roughly 110,000 inhabitants, and around 180,000 in Peoria County. Peoria is blessed with a gorgeous natural landscape, the Illinois River Valley, shaped by glaciers in the Ice Age, that left valleys and breathtaking bluffs. The Peoria Park District has almost 9,000 acres of multiple parks to treasure. Peoria is a city that feels like a small-town community, with great jobs and affordable housing by any standard, with so much to offer for people living, visiting, and playing here. There's tons of culture, festivals, shopping, nature, and amazing locally owned, non-chain restaurants and boutiques.

Whether you are an avid outdoor enthusiast and would enjoy our parks and nature reserves, canoeing or kayaking along the scenic Illinois River, Banner Marsh, or the Emiquon National Wildlife Refuge; or you love sports and would enjoy a baseball game at Dozer Park, or hockey with the Peoria Rivermen at the Peoria Civic Center; or love historic Victorian mansions built by the whiskey barons in Peoria's time as the "Whiskey Capital of the World"; or would enjoy our large group of art galleries, farmers markets, or have fun playing in the trendy Warehouse District, there is something for everyone, I promise.

So please, as an invitation from me on behalf of my beloved Peoria, grab the book and meander through the pages at your leisure. I challenge you to find some of the pieces of Peoria that would entice you to visit, and make your list of things to do in Peoria before you die. But please trust me, as a lifelong Peorian: The opportunities for great experiences are far greater than this list.

• •

Connected Restaurant
Photo courtesy of Troy Ummel

FOOD AND DRINK

ENJOY TRULY FARM-TO-CUP COFFEE
AT CAFE SANTA ROSA

Colombian-grown coffee beans journey from farm to cup at Cafe Santa Rosa. It is one of the only coffee shops in the United States that owns the coffee farm that provides the coffee beans for their cafe. The owners are both from Colombia and live and work in Peoria. Their farm is in the Cauca region of Colombia. A few years ago, they decided to open up Cafe Santa Rosa in Junction City in Peoria. They are a coffee business with a conscience: They pay their employees in Colombia a living wage, provide free health clinics, and are working to start a daycare on-site at the farm, which is 25 acres and has over 60,000 coffee trees grown in a socially/environmentally friendly way. The coffee beans are roasted in Peoria. Support this business and enjoy delicious coffee, espresso, or cappuccino.

5901 N Prospect Rd., 309-214-9255
cafesantarosa.co

TIP
Go eat a delicious dinner across the road at Cyd's in the Park.
5805 N Knoxville Ave., cyds.biz

IF YOU LOVE COFFEE, CHECK OUT SOME OTHER POPULAR SPOTS

Cultured Grounds
456 Fulton St., 309-431-7696

The Spot Coffee
9901 N Knoxville Ave., Ste. A, 309-686-0898
thespotcoffee.com

Zion Coffee Bar
803 SW Adams St., 309-670-0921
zioncoffeeco.com

thirty-thirty Coffee Co.
734 Main St., 309-713-2983
thirty-thirtycoffee.com

Leaves 'n Beans
4800 N Prospect Rd., 309-688-7685
lnbcoffee.com

Garden Street Cafe
1317 W Garden St., 309-673-4150
facebook.com/gardenstreetcafe1317

[CxT] Roasting Company
6035 Knoxville Ave., Ste. 101, 872-333-2987
cxt.coffee

MEET THE PATRON SAINT OF CHEESECAKE BAKING
AT TRIPLE DIPPLE'S

One could travel anywhere in the United States, and the gourmet cheesecakes made at Triple Dipple's will stand with a crown of glory at the top of the list of desserts and delicacies. Famous for their Sweet Tater Cheese, they also offer Oreo, Turtle, Strawberry, Original, and a featured specialty flavor that rotates every two weeks if it's something to write home to Momma about. One review claims that Triple Dipple's is the patron saint of cheesecake baking. Located just a few miles north of Peoria in Historic Downtown Second Street in Chillicothe, Triple Dipple's is an award-winning bakery that specializes in gourmet cheesecakes, cookies, and oatmeal cream pies. The proprietors began baking cheesecakes at home in their own oven, and expanded to a storefront, where they bake over 300 mini cheesecakes in a variety of flavors daily. They sell thousands of cheesecakes each month. You can also find them at farmers markets, special events, and several shops.

940 N 2nd St., Chillicothe, 309-340-9540
tripledipples.com

GO AROUND THE WORLD WITH MIDWESTERN HOSPITALITY
AT ONE WORLD CAFE

One World Cafe is located in the heart of Peoria's West Bluff, near Bradley University at 1245 West Main Street, and serves savory, globally inspired flavors and dishes that draw in a crowd regularly from all walks of life. Just a few blocks away from Peoria's downtown business district, the cafe features epic world characters muraled both outside and inside the historic brick building. There's a bar, outdoor seating, and featured art by local artists as well. The staff is more than welcoming, and the food is always delicious. They offer delicious coffee drinks and breakfast, and both the hummus and spinach artichoke dip are to die for! The menu has burgers, salads, and pizza, and you can't go wrong with their fish tacos served fried, blackened, or broiled on tortillas with veggies and fresh salsa with chips. There are plenty of vegan and gluten-sensitive menu highlights you can enjoy.

1245 W Main St., 309-672-1522
oneworld-cafe.com

TIPS

Take a walk just a few blocks away down the historic High Wine District, see all of the mansions that once belonged to barons of whiskey distilling, and meander through Giant Oak Park, with a tree believed to be over 300 years old! Some of the branches stretch out over 100 feet, and the trunk is around 13 feet in diameter. There is a picnic table, and views of the historic Easton Fountain as well.

Radish Kitchen
For more vegan options, try out One World Cafe's neighbor, Radish Kitchen, across the street in the Campustown Shopping Center for tons of vegan meals.
1200 W Main St., 309-839-2776
radishkitchen.org

Dac's Smokehouse BBQ
For the meat lovers, check out another neighbor in Campustown.
1200 W Main St., Store 11, 309-643-1223
dacspeoria.com

TAKE THE BEEFEATER CHALLENGE
AT PEORIA'S ALEXANDER'S STEAKHOUSE!

Alexander's is one of Peoria's premier steakhouses, offering an "American-style cookout" meal for you. Located in a beautiful historic brick building on the Illinois River, the grill's aromas greet you upon your arrival, and it just keeps getting better! Walk in and see the delicious, fresh salad bar and the large grill. Some steaks offered are the Porterhouse at 25-27 ounces, an 18-ounce T-bone, and of course the New York strip, ribeye, sirloin, or filet mignon. All steaks are hand-cut daily by their in-house butchers! For the brave who order the Beefeater, a three-pound top sirloin, the challenge is to eat the steak in one hour. There's also a trip to the salad bar, one side, and a grilled piece of Texas toast. Winners get their choice of a $20 gift card or an Alexander's T-shirt that states, "Last night I had the best piece of meat in town."

100 Alexander Ave., 309-688-0404
alexanderssteak.com

Jim's Steakhouse is reminiscent of a place the famous members of the Rat Pack would choose to hang out and dine, play the piano, and order exquisite steaks and cocktails. It's overloaded with ambience, very elegant, and offers delicious steaks. It is located smack-dab in the middle of downtown Peoria, known for consistently decadent food and live music at the piano bar every weekend.
110 SW Jefferson Ave., 309-673-5300
jimssteakhouse.net

The **Lariat Steakhouse** is another iconic Peoria steakhouse with great ambience and excellent food, locally owned since the1940s.
2232 W Glen Ave., 309-691-4731
peoriasteakhouse.com

Love meat? Get some delicious BBQ meats at The **Smo-King Pit Bar-B-Que**. They brag about their St. Louis-style ribs, and they have every right! Locally owned and operated by Michael and Michelle Citchens, the Smo-King Pit showcases Michael's southern Mississippi upbringing and love for BBQ. The BBQ meats, ribs, and rib tips are hand-rubbed with their special Smo-King Pit meat rub and then smoked, depending upon the meats, for three hours. The beef brisket and pork butts get smoked for 10 hours!
2200 W War Memorial Dr., 309-688-3606
smo-kingpit.com

PARTAKE
OF THE ANNUAL ITOO SHISH-KA-BOB & LEBANESE CUISINE EVENT

The Itoo Society was established in 1914 in Peoria, joining Lebanese immigrants from Aytou, Lebanon, as a social and community group. They quickly began to work as a charitable organization as well, and purchased Itoo Hall for social functions and as a rental venue. The Lebanese community in Peoria is vast and has thrived for over a century. For over 50 years, the Itoo Society has held several events, including the annual Itoo Shish-Ka-Bob & Lebanese Cuisine event.

It is traditionally held on the last Sunday of June, and includes meals with a choice of a chicken or beef kabob! Sides include authentic Lebanese cabbage rolls, pita bread, and salad. It is extremely popular. It offers dining in the large Itoo Hall, and outdoor seating in the pavilion. Carryouts are available. Catch the annual Itoo Supper in November.

Itoo Society and Banquet Hall
4909 W Farmington Rd., 309-676-9725
itoosociety.org
itoohall.com

TIP

Looking for a FANTASTIC Lenten Fish Fry? Holy Family Parish has the best dang fish fry in Peoria! They host their delicious fish fry each Friday of Lent from 4-7 p.m. Choice of catfish, walleye, Parmesan-crusted tilapia, baked cod, or shrimp dinners, which come with baked potato or French fries and coleslaw (cheese pizza for the kiddos). Orders must be made in person or online only.

2329 W Reservoir Blvd.

ENJOY UPSCALE DINING
AT JONAH'S SEAFOOD HOUSE

With beautiful Illinois River views, you can spy the skyline of Peoria and the lighted bridge as well at Jonah's 2601 Oyster Bar while you sample the fresh-shucked oysters or a martini. Offering the finest of fresh seafood and delicious steaks, Jonah's will ensure you enjoy every minute of your dining experience. The jumbo coconut shrimp appetizer with a slightly spicy, yet sweet, honey sauce will complement your meal whether you order surf or turf. Since the seafood is fresh, the menu changes, but should marlin or mahi-mahi be on the menu, try it grilled, or try the blackened salmon and pair it with a delicious glass of wine. Don't forget about the Market & Bake Shop, where you can purchase appetizers, clam chowder, gumbo, salads, Jonah's dinner meal kits with steak and seafood options, and cocktails to go.

2601 N Main St., East Peoria, 309-694-0946
jonahsseafood.com

TIP
Follow the Meanwhile Back in Peoria blog to find fun and informative things about Peoria and great places to eat! meanwhilebackinpeoria.com

CELEBRATE BLISSFUL DELISH
AT TREFZGER'S BAKERY

Going back to 1861 and the Civil War, Simon Trefzger held a contract with the Union troops for all of their baked goods. Today, Trefzger's Bakery holds strong with the tradition of caring about their clientele's needs. It is the oldest bakery in Central Illinois, and deserves the bragging rights as one of the best. It is located in a historic brick building at 4416 North Prospect Road, in downtown Peoria Heights, and is exquisite, with wood beams, brick walls, and glass cases showcasing delicious cupcakes, cookies, and pies. Get your orders in as soon as possible for your special-event cakes, but feel free to swing by on a whim, and get a cookie with the most delicious frosting you have tasted, and have a cup of coffee. They offer specialty cakes, king Cakes, orange chiffon, and made-to-order cakes. Other items include their tasty cinnamon rolls, pumpkin pies, delicious donuts, and cream horns!

4416 N Prospect Rd., 309-685-9221
trefzgersbakery.com

A BOTTLE OF RED, A BOTTLE OF WHITE
BECKON AT PAPARAZZI RESTAURANT

Just like Billy Joel's classic hit song, "Scenes from an Italian Restaurant," Paparazzi Restaurant will surely remind you of the perfect ambience in an Italian restaurant. Tucked away on a hidden side street, but not too far from the hustle and bustle of a thriving neighborhood, Paparazzi's will steal your appetite and heart. Reservations are highly recommended, and once you arrive and walk inside, the ambience is enchanting. Green walls sport numerous old Hollywood films and actors highlighted in frames all around. Food is ordered a la carte, and features many appetizers and a pasta section where you can choose your pasta, sauce, and any add-ons to your personalized concoction. There are entrees such as shrimp scampi, Veal Paparazzi, chicken cacciatore, and of course delicious bottles of wine, ranging in price from $16.50 to $40. Paparazzi is small and elegant, and you'll find your favorite bottle of red or white.

4315 N Voss St., Peoria Heights, 309-682-5205
paparazzipeoriaheights.com

TAKE ME TO CHURCH, AN OLD CHURCH, TO EAT AND DRINK:
OBED & ISAAC'S MICROBREWERY AND EATERY

Obed & Isaac's was originally an old church that was built in 1889, and is unique, with beautiful stones, stunning wood, and stained glass on the outside, and statues on the inside. The original church was designed in the Richardsonian Romanesque Revival style, housed numerous churches throughout the century, and was later an event venue, business offices, and finally Obed & Isaac's. Beautifully and historically preserved, the interior is stunning, and you can eat outside on the patio and in the beer garden. The restaurant features your choice of your favorite craft brews, made on-site at the brewery. Located in downtown Peoria, and just a few blocks away from the Illinois River, you can enjoy delicious food. This establishment is pet-friendly, pets are allowed in the beer garden and bocce garden. Obed & Isaac's is also bicycle-friendly, and you can challenge your friends to a game of bocce or bags in the beer garden as well.

321 NE Madison Ave., 309-306-0190
obedandisaacs.com

HERE ARE SOME OTHER GREAT OPTIONS FOR DINING IN DOWNTOWN PEORIA

Sugar Wood-Fired Bistro & Gourmet Treats
Smell the delicious wood fires as you walk up to the establishment. They offer made-from-scratch, wood-fired pizzas and sandwiches. Simple, casual, and delicious, with indoor and outdoor seating.
826 SW Adams St., 309-676-0848
sugarpeoria.com

Rhythm Kitchen Music Cafe
A cool restaurant/bar with live music and an eclectic global menu. It is located near the riverfront in downtown Peoria and has great energy and a hip vibe.
305 SW Water St., 309-676-9668
rhythmkitchenmusiccafe.com

Ulrich's Rebellion Room
Get one of the best burgers in town along with beer at this Irish pub that happens to be open until 4 a.m. on weekends in downtown Peoria. Fun decor, fun crowds! Great carryout, too.
631 Main St., 309-676-1423
ulrichsrebellionroom.com

WELCOME TO
WATER STREET
AT KELLEHER'S IRISH PUB & EATERY

Kelleher's is a beautiful eatery in downtown Peoria in a historic building, with lovely Irish decor. Some unique features are the atrium and fireplace. Dine with a wonderful river view, and enjoy outdoor dining in nice weather. Head to Kelleher's on St. Patrick's Day and enjoy Irish dancers and some live music. This is a family-friendly event, and kids can get their faces painted and go home with animal balloons. Enjoy some traditional Irish dishes such as shepherd's pie, bangers and mash, Guinness pot roast, or their delicious homemade chicken pot pie, yummy! Even runners can celebrate the luck of the Irish in the Blarney Blitz 5k Run and Walk! Specialty burgers include the Irish Burger, the Dublin Steak Burger, Trinity Sandwich, corned beef, and the Tipperary Toastie, an Irish BLT served with a choice of melted cheese, served on sourdough. Kelleher's has a nice selection of craft beer, and Irish bourbons, too.

619 SW Water St., 309-673-6000
kellehersonwater.com

MORE PUB EXPERIENCES

Donnelly's Irish Pub
A multi-generational, locally and family-owned Irish pub, Donnelly's has the decor of an authentic Irish pub, with a beautiful wood bar and wood throughout the establishment. It is great for a date night or a big family gathering. Delicious sandwiches, Irish fare, and tons of craft beer on tap are available, along with friendly service and indoor and outdoor seating.
4501 N Rockwood Dr., 309-681-0800
donnellyspubpeoria.com

The Fox Pub and Cafe
The Fox Pub has a British theme, and has delicious craft ales. Get your bangers and mash, and fish and chips, cottage pie, and Buckingham's Bacon-Bleu Mac and Cheese.
7800 N Sommer St., Ste. 302, 309-692-3693
thefoxpubandcafe.com

DON'T BE A JERK, EAT AUTHENTIC CARIBBEAN CUISINE
AT THE JERK HUT RESTAURANT!

When a love for Caribbean cooking partners with a native Jamaican chef with decades of experience, you will see the recipe for culinary excellence and success. Traditional jerk entrees such as pork, chicken, and ribs will give you jerk entrees served with red beans, rice, plus two sides to fill your belly. Fill in the sides with Southern cuisine: mac and cheese, collard greens, cabbage, spicy mac and cheese, candied yams, and of course the red beans and rice. Do you have family or friends visiting with you who are vegan or vegetarian? They serve vegetarian dishes and meat-free dishes, including meatless tofu and jackfruit substitute; get the jerk tofu tacos with fries, jerk veggie burger, or jerk tofu bowl! Oh, spicy! Get their curry chicken, goat, or shrimp, or get your jerk on with the jerk chicken sandwich, jerk catfish sandwich, or jerk pork chop sandwich.

1200 W Main St., Unit 21A, 309-966-3325
jerkhutpeoria.com

SAVOR FLAVORFUL AND FRESH FOOD
AT THANH LIHN
VIETNAMESE RESTAURANT

Authentic Vietnamese cuisine may be found on Main Street at Thanh Lihn. Enjoy their fresh lunch buffet Monday through Saturday from 11 a.m. to 3 p.m., and dinner buffet Fridays and Saturdays from 4 to 8:30 p.m. Thanh Lihn has pretty decor and nice service, and ample portions for meals. Standout crabmeat rangoon, tofu or avocado spring rolls, and shrimp/pork spring rolls come wrapped in rice paper and stuffed with cilantro, lettuce, vermicelli, and a special hoisin peanut sauce. Grilled lemongrass chicken is served with Vietnamese relish, veggies, rice, and sweet soy sauce. There's also spicy lemongrass beef/pork, spicy lemongrass tofu with rice, and more. For stir-fry noodles you have a choice of crunchy noodles and can substitute any meat with tofu, and also add extra meat or extra veggies for an additional cost. There are tons of choices of noodle soups, thick or thin rice noodle entrees, and even some curry— Vietnamese chicken curry, green curry with bamboo, green beans, green peppers, eggplant, basil, and coconut milk, with choice of meat or tofu as well.

1209 W Main St., 309-495-0179
thanhlinhvietnameserestaurant.com

DINE NEAR A 30-FOOT-TALL, INDOOR WATERFALL
AT CONNECTED RESTAURANT

The saying "Don't judge a book by its cover" rings true here, as the exterior of this restaurant is plain, but once you walk inside it is another story, with elegant decor, soft, romantic lighting, atmospheric faux shop windows, and four private dining rooms. The Waterfall Room features a 30-foot-tall waterfall, Chandelier Room, Fireplace Room, and the Vault. It is an Italian American restaurant. House specials include the Costata Di Vitello, which is a bone-in veal chop with fresh seasonings; the Bistecca Al Barolo, a filet mignon in a Barolo wine sauce with caramelized pearl onions and mushrooms; and the Cinghiale, wild boar tenderloin served with a pepper crust in an Indonesian lemon, ginger, and sweet soy sauce. Try one of their lemon basil martinis. Birthday patrons will receive a red rose, and desserts for anniversaries and birthdays come out with a sparkling candle. Truly one of the very best Peoria has to offer for a romantic, delicious, and welcoming evening.

3218 N Dries Ln., 309-686-5925
connectedpeoria.com

OTHER RESTAURANTS TO TRY

2Chez
Swing by for The Brubaker, which is smoked in cherrywood, and has Old Forester bourbon, Campari, fresh lemon, and a house-made syrup.
7815 N Knoxville Ave.
2chezrestaurant.com

Hearth
4604 N Prospect Rd., Peoria Heights, 309-686-0234
hearthpeoria.com

Thyme Kitchen and Craft Beer
736 SW Washington St., 309-713-2619
thymepeoria.com

Jim's Bistro
4612 N Prospect Rd., Peoria Heights, 309-682-9219
jimsbistropeoriaheights.com

GET SEAFOOD FROM AROUND THE WORLD
AT THE FISH HOUSE PEORIA

Serving fresh seafood, steak, chicken, and pasta since 1976, the Fish House restaurant holds a solid reputation for delicious food, and offers a classic lounge to enjoy your favorite beer and wine. Enjoy baked Oysters Rockefeller or try some fried alligator for a starter! Grab a cup of New England clam chowder or lobster bisque as well, before your entree. There are several choices for lobster and king crab, and some surf and turf entrees, with an African lobster tail and filet mignon cooked to perfection. Fifteen-plus choices for seafood entrees are available, such as Halibut Florentine, Atlantic salmon, Broiled Neptune's Platter with lobster, gulf shrimp, bay scallops, tilapia and a deviled crab cake! But wait! The Fish House has daily fish specials as well that vary depending on availability: Hawaiian big eye tuna, sweet chile Thai sea bass, Tuscan or Hawaiian mahi-mahi and Tuscan halibut. You can also purchase fresh seafood at the seafood market in the back of the building! Open daily.

4919 N University St., 309-691-9358
fishhousepeoria.com

COOL OFF
AT YENI'S PALARTE ICE CREAM SHOP

A Mexican ice cream parlor, Yeni's Palarte Ice Cream Shop is where batches of ice cream are made on-site with fresh ingredients! There are more than 70 feature flavors, rotating each week throughout the year. In addition to traditional homemade Mexican ice creams, the alcohol-infused ice creams infused ice creams and slushies include special flavors made with amaretto stone sour and Fireball whiskey, holiday specials such as Irish cream for St. Patrick's Day, and some made with champagne and wine. Non-infused flavors include queso blackberry, purple rain, birthday cake, praline bacon, and—don't forget the slushies—raspados/fruit slushies. Or, order an agua fresca like Jamaica or horchata. It's locally owned and operated by dynamic duo business partners, Yeni Rodriguez and Chris McCall.

4303 N Prospect Rd., Peoria Heights, 309-966-0228

TRY AUTHENTIC LEBANESE MEDITERRANEAN FOOD
AT RESTAURANT KABAB-G'S

Simple, uncomplicated, and pure deliciousness awaits at Kabab-G's. Hummus delights include one made with crushed garbanzo beans, garlic, and olive oil with pita bread, and hummus with meat and pine nuts—shawarma beef, pine nuts on hummus with pita bread. Simple, see? Tons of options are available for meat lovers and vegetarians as well, including seven options of its namesake—kabobs with beef, chicken, kafta, cheese, vegetable, lamb, or the "combo" with a choice of three served on hummus and salad. There are also bone-in lamb chops, salmon, mahi-mahi grilled with secret seasonings, grilled veggies, hummus, salad, and rice, too! Shawarma beef or chicken is marinated and slow-roasted. Falafels, fatteh kabsa, tabouli, ful beans, and delicious homemade yogurt with cucumber round out the offerings. Get your cabbage rolls here, and traditional Lebanese salad. Little ones can get their kabob for $5 and, for dessert, baklava! Small, simple, and great personalized service are yours at Kabab-G.

7800 N Sommer St., Ste. 610, 309-691-6188

OTHER MIDDLE EASTERN RESTAURANTS TO TRY

Haddad's Restaurant
7805 N University St., 309-966-4296

Jerusalem Restaurant
2027 W Farmington Rd., Ste. B, 309-863-2186

Chef Moussa
201 E Lake Ave., 309-966-4234

STIR UP TACOS, TEQUILA, AND PUNCH
AT CAYENNE RESTAURANT

Tacos with a twist, and made fresh from scratch, give Cayenne an edge over other restaurants, with 14 taco options. One option is the Quesabirria, which comes with marinated brisket and shredded cheese, red onion, cilantro, and consomme. A vegetarian option is the Leaf Eater, featuring chipotle-barbecued jackfruit, vegan mozzarella cheese, guacamole, black bean salsa, and tortilla strips. Other tantalizing dishes are the Mexican taco salad and smothered brisket burrito, and there are custom-order dishes as well. Cayenne is filled with a fun mural painting by a local artist and inspired by Dia de los Muertos, or the Day of the Dead. There's an extensive tequila list and handcrafted cocktails: try the Blue Heat with Casa Amigos Blanco. House margaritas can't be beat, with fresh-squeezed lime and lemon juice, shaken or stirred! "Boozy Punches" that are house-made and available on draft with fresh-squeezed juice are the House Sangria and Island Boy with Rum.

4542 N Prospect Rd., Peoria Heights, 309-966-1035
cayennepeoria.com

MORE LOCAL MEXICAN CUISINE FAVORITES

Mi Familia Restaurant
Delicious food awaits. Grab some chicken or steak fajitas, or an enchilada dinner that comes with rice and beans. Homemade chips and salsa are made in house! It's a small neighborhood restaurant, reasonably priced, with dine-in or takeout.
2007 N Wisconsin Ave., #2625, 309-685-8477

El Mexicano Restaurant
A tiny little Mexican restaurant that packs its power in delicious food! Burritos, chimichangas, fish tacos, and more.
1520 NE Jefferson St., 309-636-8858

Los Cabos Cantina and Grill
A bright and festive restaurant with very friendly service. The rice is delicious, and their tacos and quesadillas are to die for! Great choices of appetizers and entrees, and the kids' menu is a plus! Gourmet Mexican seafood dishes, and fabulous margaritas!
7800 N Sommer St., #106, 309-692-2710
loscabospeoria.com

EAT A HOT DOG
AT LOU'S DRIVE-IN

With curb service with a carhop, just like the good old days of the drive-in diner, Lou's Drive-In is a summertime favorite for folks in Peoria. Sit at the counter along the exterior of the building, or sit at one of the patio tables with your kiddos. Order a delicious mug of their famous homemade root beer to wash down your hot dog or burger! Lou's is open seasonally between May and September, and has been a fixture for over 50 years. The food is simple, but delicious, served in paper containers. You can get tenderloins, burgers, hot dogs, chili dogs, add some cheese, too, and get some chili cheese fries, also. There are amazing, old-fashioned malts, shakes, and root beer floats, and believe it or not, root beer to-go in a quart, half-gallon, or gallon container! The bright neon light will beckon you to drive on in.

4229 N Knoxville Ave., 309-685-4519
facebook.com/lousdrivein

FOLKS WHO LOVE
LOU'S DRIVE-IN WILL ALSO ENJOY

Emo's Dairy Mart
Offering seasonal outdoor service of ice cream and hot dogs, with an iconic clown head on top of the building. Ice cream treats and slushies are offered, cash-only, and several patio tables are available.
3618 N Prospect Rd.

Theo's Ice Cream
Open year-round, Theo's has Peoria's best chili-cheese dog, hands down! Also, delicious ice cream treats, shakes, and frozen ice cream cakes.
3633 N Gale Ave., 309-688-5854

The Ice Cream Shack
A seasonal hot dog and ice cream stand with outdoor eating, cash-only.
2313 NE Adams St., 309-686-2828

PICK A PIZZA
AT AGATUCCI'S

The Agatucci family's Peoria connection was brought about over a century ago, when an Italian immigrant named Vincenzo Agatucci came to the city and opened a family business in 1926. It evolved over the years, turning into an Italian restaurant and pizzeria in the 1940s. They developed delicious spaghetti and other dishes, and perfected one of Peoria's favorite pizza joints.

The establishment is casual and is a great place to have a drink with buddies at the bar, or to bring your large family in for delicious food and a fun atmosphere. It's a classic Peoria joint, with a regular clientele, but always welcoming to newcomers. They have it all, from fried chicken to pasta and burgers. Pizza comes in small or large, and don't forget to order their famous Tiger Sauce, which is a zesty garlic sauce to dip pizza in.

2607 N University St., 309-688-8200
agatuccis.com

PIZZA LOVERS WILL ENJOY THESE

Castaways Bar and Grill
1707 N 4th St., Chillicothe, 309-274-3484
castawayschillicothe.com

Fedora's Pizza & Gyros
1229 W McClure Ave., #1, 309-685-4976
facebook.com/fedoraspizza

Brienzo's Wood Fired Pizza
4450 N Prospect Rd., Peoria Heights, 309-966-4185
brienzospizza.com

Veteran's Pub & Pizza
2525 NE Adams St., 309-713-3029

UNWIND
AT A PIZZA JOINT AND BLUES BAR ON ADAMS

Jack's On Adams is a pizza joint and a blues bar located in the heart of Peoria's downtown, blocks away from the exciting Warehouse District. Owner Jack Berres was born and raised in Peoria, and wanted to own a business in Downtown Peoria for quite some time, and has brought that dream to reality with this extraordinary establishment. He brought his expertise that he learned in the restaurant business while living for a time in St. Petersburg, Florida, and shares that excitement with Peorians. There is live blues music every Friday and Saturday night from 8:30 p.m. to 11:30 p.m., and delicious cocktails and of course, tavern style pizza, which is a classic Peoria favorite. There are Happy Hours that run from 9 p.m. to 1 a.m. on Mondays through Thursdays as well. The menu is expanding currently, and don't forget to check out their Facebook page for all of the specials and events section to catch what blues band you won't want to miss.

107 SW Adams St., 309-839-2855
jacksonadamspeoria.com

EXPLORE A HISTORIC LOCATION
AT THE BLUE DUCK BARBECUE TAVERN

This tavern enjoys a deep history on Peoria's riverfront: It was the original site for the Rock Island Depot, formerly known as the River Station, built in 1899. Older Peorians remember riding the "Peoria Rocket" to Chicago until it closed down in 1978. It is listed on the National Register of Historic Places. There are large-scale efforts to foster the resurgence of downtown Peoria. The unique venue is part of what makes Downtown Peoria special, and unlike any other. The interior has antique barn wood on the walls, beautiful art, and newer additions to lighting, sound, and TVs. Do you love pork butts? Well, you have found the perfect place for perfect pork butts. In the bar you can order draft beers from local microbreweries, and an imported whiskey selection. Food is made from scratch! Enjoy specialty smoked meats, BBQ, and wings.

212 SW Water St., 309-981-5801
blueduckbarbecue.com

TIP

Take a quick walk down the riverfront to see the Dan Fogelberg Memorial at Riverfront Park. Dan was born and raised in Peoria and rose to epic heights as a musician. You are probably familiar with the hit songs "Leader of the Band," "Same Old Lang Syne," and "Missing You." 100 Morton St.

WET YOUR WHISTLE IN A REALLY NICE DIVE BAR IN A GARAGE
AT MIKE'S TAVERN

What was once a stag bar, opened in the 1930s with standing room only in an old garage, has been reborn into a really nice dive bar in a garage! Mike's Tavern, a favorite place to grab a beer for generations, has been refurbished but also kept much of what made this dive so awesome! The ceiling has the original tin tiles, and there are a handful of old school desks to sit on, which used to be the only seating. They kept the classic pay phone, and there is a pretty neat collection of old beer cans, including Billy Beer! A lit-up barber pole and some vintage signs have been added as well. Don't miss the room at the back that has gaming and a dartboard. They have added a kitchen, so you can munch while you drink! The food selection offers tenderloins and burgers, with the option to add tater tots to any sandwich.

626 N Cedar Ave., West Peoria, 309-674-1860

NEARBY WATERING HOLES

Castle's Patio Inn
802 W Loucks Ave., 309-685-9570

The Owl's Nest
2128 W Callender Ave., West Peoria, 309-676-0853
facebook.com/matwil17

Tartan Inn
428 N Waverly Ave., West Peoria, 309-966-2444
facebook.com/tartaninn

Getaway
321 N Western Ave., West Peoria, 309-637-1178

West Town Tap
515 N Western Ave., 309-839-0576
westtowntap.com

Racks on the Rocks
2800 W Farmington Rd., 309-839-2609
facebook.com/racksonrocks

The Fieldhouse Bar & Grill
1200 W Main St., #24, 309-494-9600
fieldhousepeoria.com

Tina's Coach Stop
3522 W Lincoln Ave., 309-676-5150

The Basket Case
610 W Main St., 309-676-2273

Club Diesel
629 Main St.
facebook.com/dieselpeoria

MUSIC
AND ENTERTAINMENT

A CITY WITHIN A CITY: SCAMPERS UNITE
AT THE SUMMER CAMP MUSIC FESTIVAL

Summer Camp Music Festival has taken place at Three Sisters Park over Memorial Day weekend for the past two decades in Chillicothe, Illinois, just 15 minutes north of Peoria. People from all over the country bring their camping gear and supplies needed to camp and enjoy the three-day-long music celebration. The annual festival now brings in more than 20,000 people to enjoy tons of bands that play on seven stages over the three days. There is a variety of music genres including electronic dance music (EDM), blues, jazz, folk, and band jams. There are hoopers, vendors selling jewelry, art, statues, exhibits, and food and drink vendors as well. Soulpatch, a permanent garden space at Three Sisters Park, helps give you an "immersive experience" of art, such as their Illumination Woods, that gives you an art experience with movement and colors and nature. You can get henna tattoos and enjoy workshops and sunrise yoga, have a wild time dancing, and feel like you're at a hippie fest.

summercampfestival.com

OTHER FESTIVALS
Peoria Blues and Heritage Music Festival
Tailgate N' Tallboys Music Festival

SMASH A TV
AT GONE MAD RAGE ROOM

Feeling some angst or stress from pressures at work? Book your turn at the Gone Mad Rage Room and smash like Wreck-It Ralph! Pick your tunes, go over the rules to keep you safe, and custom pick what you smash. TVs or a dress? No problem! They will give you some thick coveralls, gloves, and a helmet with a face shield. Wear closed shoes and pull long hair back. When you go online to pick your package, there are numerous options for things to DESTROY! There are a few price/package choices for you to CRUSH, such as Bring Your Own Stuff (BYOS), which is for two people, with 15 minutes of one box of anything to bring in to smash. The top of the line is "The Break Up" where you can have 40 things to smash in 30 minutes, and they will even write the name of the "ex" on each item you get to destroy. Enjoy the destruction and leave fulfilled!

1001 SW Washington St., Ste. 5-201, 309-419-2461
gonemadrageroom.com

THROW THAT AXE
AT GONE AXE THROWING

Experience fun with your friends throwing down axes in "a public lane" or "a private lane." You know your night is going to be a blast when players need to sign a waiver and go through the safety course with the "Axe Master," who will go over the rules and process to maximize fun and safety. Gone Axe Throwing is the perfect event to book a private party, and the price is based on the number of people and how long you plan to reserve the lane. Staff will monitor but not limit alcohol so, as in the safety course, common sense will count a long way toward having an exciting evening. There are lots of choices of appetizers, delicious flatbreads, especially the chicken bacon ranch flatbread, and nine flavor options for wings. I recommend being on time, and definitely make reservations ahead of time to ensure maximum time and fun!

1001 SW Washington St., Ste. 5-201, 309-419-2461
goneaxethrowing.com

MORE FUN FOR GROWNUPS!
8 Bit Arcade Bar Peoria
100 State St., Ste. 1a, 309-713-3007
8bitbeercade.com

Par-A-Dice Hotel and Casino
21 Blackjack Blvd., East Peoria, 309-699-7711
paradicecasino.com

JOIN
THE ILLINOIS VALLEY YACHT AND CANOE CLUB—IVY CLUB

The Ivy Club has been an integral part of boaters in Peoria for 100 years. It is located along the Illinois River, in front of a section of the river called Peoria Lake. It is a not-for-profit boating and social organization. The Ivy Club's beautiful and historic facility has a really nice harbor with a panoramic view of the water. Boaters can enjoy the great restaurant and bar. Visitors are welcome to come to any events held at the Ivy Club regularly! There is an outdoor swimming pool, and swim lessons are offered. You can see sailboat racing, an event called the Ivy Club Kids Cardboard Boat Race, lots of cookouts, and even a tiki bar at the pool. The harbor has boat slips, a fuel dock with gas and diesel, and a pump out. Attend the Annual Pig Roast in September, and a special St. Patrick's Day celebration.

5102 N Galena Rd., Peoria Heights, 309-682-5419
ivyclub.org

CLIMB A 20,000-SQUARE-FOOT WAREHOUSE
AT FIRST ASCENT PEORIA

Located in Peoria's Historic Warehouse District, a group of Peoria climbers and First Ascent Climbing & Fitness took an old steel supply warehouse and turned it into 20,000 square feet for climbers of all levels. This is a combination fitness center, yoga studio, and what's claimed to be a "full-service climbing gym." Purchase a day pass, and if you are new to climbing or have not been climbing in a long time, it is recommended that you purchase a Guided Climbing Session that will give you guidance on all the things you will need to know for safe climbing. The main thing you will need once you have your day pass and session are shoes, harness, and chalk for climbing. If you are visiting Peoria with your kids, they offer several kids' climbing classes and even a summer camp that has different fun themes each day, with new skills taught throughout the camp.

927 SW Washington St., 309-966-0831
faclimbing.com/peoria

MORE ADVENTURES

Gone in 60 Escape Rooms

This amusement center in downtown Peoria offers games that force the group to match wits to solve the puzzles and escape! You must solve the puzzle in 60 minutes or less!

1001 SW Washington St., 309-419-2461

gonein60.com

Elevate Trampoline Park

Kids and parents alike can have a blast jumping at Elevate Trampoline Park. There are also dodgeball pits and foam pits. You can also participate in Galaxy Laser Tag inside as well!

8800 N Allen Rd., 309-966-0231

elevatetrampolineparkpeoria.com/contact

Round One

Kids, and kids at heart, will love this amazing, fun facility. It offers bowling, karaoke, billiards, and ping-pong! There are arcade games, darts, and food! There are also beer and wine for the grownups, so sit while you take a breather from all the entertainment.

2200 W War Memorial Dr., 309-822-5353

round1usa.com

Bass Pro Shop

A great place to visit and shop: Get your camping and boating gear! See some cool freshwater fish in a giant tank. Bring the kids to bowl and eat dinner at Uncle Buck's Fish Bowl and Grill!

1000 Bass Pro Shops Dr., East Peoria, 309-427-3300

unclebucksfishbowlandgrill.com

Hooked On Fishing

This private park and nonprofit teaches fishing education to kids ages 5-15, and to senior citizens. It is open to the public on Sundays during warm months and by reservation in summer months. Fishing is catch-and-release, and Hooked On Fishing teaches fishing techniques, ecology, and how to keep water supplies healthy.

1807 N Main St., East Peoria, 309-219-3560

hookedonfishingpark.org

TAKE TIME TO PLAY AND EXPLORE
AT THE PEORIA PLAYHOUSE CHILDREN'S MUSEUM

Bring your littles to the six permanent exhibits and other fun rotating programs. Kids can learn about what Peoria was like from the past, present, and future in the Peoria, Then and Now exhibit. For the dinosaur and fossil lovers, the Fossil Rocks exhibit allows them to explore through fossil activities, learn about prehistoric eras, and touch real fossils from millions of years ago. Learn about energy, speed, and force with the Motion Commotion exhibit, visit the Family Farm exhibit, and get hands-on playing with real tools at the All Construction Great and Small exhibit. The museum is handicapped-accessible, but they kindly ask for strollers to be left outside. Kids will have fun in this hands-on, interactive museum located right next to the Peoria Zoo. It's geared towards children under age 12; don't forget to check out their Art Room for older kids with programs for different art each week.

2218 N Prospect Rd., 309-323-6900
peoriaplayhouse.org

TIP
Bring a picnic lunch and head over to the nearby Historic Glen Oak Park playground, with drinking fountains and picnic tables. Stroll on a walk and see the Glen Oak Lagoon!

GO ON SAFARI
AT THE WILD KINGDOM AT PEORIA ZOO

Since the 1800s, Peoria has enjoyed animals in its Peoria Park District near Glen Oak Park. Updated drastically in the 1950s, with advice from the host of *Mutual of Omaha's Wild Kingdom*, Marlin Perkins, who was the director at the St. Louis Zoo at the time, the Peoria Zoo has progressed significantly over the decades. The Peoria Zoological Society joined forces with the zoo to grow in size and exhibits. There is a wonderful Africa exhibit, where you can see diverse African animals such as red river hogs, colobus monkeys, mandrills, Thomson's gazelle, Aldabra tortoise, white rhinoceros, giraffes, zebras, and of course the African lions. Kids will enjoy the Aviary and the Australian Walk-About and see the emus, red-necked wallaby, and the black swans as well. See turtles, toads, frogs, and the Chinese alligator. They offer summer day camps that include crafts, games, and animal encounters, and each year they host the fun Howl-Zoo-Ween.

2320 N Prospect Rd., 309-686-3365
peoriazoo.org

RELAX
AT THE MACKINAW VALLEY WINERY AND VINEYARD

Located just about 20 minutes from Peoria, the Mackinaw Valley Vineyard and Winery is open year-round, and features award-winning wines from Central Illinois. They received bronze and silver medals in 2016 at the New York Finger Lakes International, the Double Gold Medal for Alexander's Conquest, and the Gold Medal for Diane's Desire at the Illinois State Fair Awards. They host fun events like Trivia Night; Music in the Tasting Room; Murder Mystery Dinner; International Music, Wine, and Craft Beer Festival; salsa dance lessons, Christmas Market, Spring Market, and Concerts in the Vineyard. See a gorgeous, 30-mile view of valleys and farms, and a tasting room with over 20 wines to taste, with the first three tastes only a buck! Enjoy 86 acres of nature and 15 acres of grapes, with many decks and walking paths. There is a bar, gift shop, and annual Grape Stomp and Harvest Festival. You are allowed to bring your own prepared food, but catering is offered with The Catering Company, 309-678-9000.

33633 State Rte. 9, Mackinaw, 309-359-9463
mackinawvalleyvineyard.com

COME SEE A SHOW
AT THE PEORIA PLAYERS THEATRE

The Peoria Players Theatre was founded in 1919, and brags that it is the oldest continuously running community theater in the state of Illinois. The Players have never closed their doors, and offer year-round, quality entertainment. The theater began at its first location at the Peoria Women's Club, which was then located in a fire station. Its current location was designed by Architect Les Kenyon in 1957, in the center of the city. You can see hit Broadway shows with stellar performances such as *The Shawshank Redemption*, *Billy Elliot*, and *Sweet Charity*, plus shows like *Rent* and more. Each Halloween you can dress up, bring approved props, and attend a midnight show of *The Rocky Horror Picture Show*; during the summer you can see the Summer Youth Theater productions, and if you are visiting Peoria during the holiday season, do not miss the Peoria Players & PAPAS (Peoria Area Performing Arts School) Holiday Special.

4300 N University St., 309-688-4473
peoriaplayers.org

TIP

Enjoy a delicious dinner and a musical or comedy show from October to April, and again in July and August at The Barn III Dinner Theatre and Event Center. The Barn III is an awesome addition to a group bus trip to the Peoria area! 1451 Timberline Rd., Goodfield, 309-965-2545 thebarnIII.com

SEE PEORIA'S OUTDOOR THEATER UNDER THE TENT
AT THE CORN STOCK THEATRE

The Corn Stock Theatre is Peoria's only outdoor theater under the tent at Bradley Park. Providing wonderful theater each summer for over 60 years, Corn Stock has brought traditional shows, classical musicals, and even some edgier more modern shows to its audiences, and have added more inclusive shows, so that people from all walks of life can participate in the theatrical experience. There is nothing more fun than to drive into Bradley Park, and walk around, enjoying some light food and even a glass of wine on a beautiful summer evening. The scene around the big tent is lovely; you can mingle with friends or other theatergoers, and grab some popcorn. Corn Stock Theatre has three theater programs, so you can watch live performances year-round: the tent in the summer, the Winter Playhouse in the Corn Stock Lab a short distance down the path of the park, and Corn Stock for Kids as well.

1700 N Park Rd., 309-676-2916
cornstocktheatre.com

OTHER THESPIAN ATTRACTIONS

Eastlight Theatre

Eastlight Theatre hosts traditional theater shows, including the annual holiday favorite, *Joseph and The Amazing Technicolor Dreamcoat*. Once a year the theater hosts the Penguin Project, which joins peer mentors with children with developmental disabilities to perform well-known Broadway musicals. Located at the Byron Moore Auditorium at East Peoria Community High School, 1401 E Washington St. East Peoria, 309-699-7469
eastlighttheatre.com

Broadway Deli & Lounge

Head to lunch Tuesday through Saturday, 11 a.m.-4 p.m., at The Waterhouse's Broadway Lounge, and enjoy live entertainment and musical shows on the weekend evenings! Delicious food and amazing shows. Don't miss shows such as the Dueling Pianos Dinner & Show, comedy acts, *Camelot*, and *The Holy Grail*!
316 SW Washington St., 309-431-9708
broadwaypeoria.com

ZOOM AROUND
THE GO-KART TRACK
AT KARTVILLE

You can't mess up fast-track fun at Kartville, which has a go-kart track, miniature golf, and more for the family. Kids age eight on up can drive the go-karts, and kids age 10 and up can power the ATVs and dune buggies. Kids of all ages can ride on the bumper boats, but must be age six to drive one by themselves. Grab one of the helmets and challenge your crew in the baseball and softball batting cages, with slow- to fast-pitch options to improve your skills. Do not forget the 18 holes for mini golf! Golf clubs for adults and kids will end your afternoon of fun. Kartville has all of your amusement park classic snacks with hot dogs, ice cream sandwiches, sno-cones, cotton candy, candy, and the handmade lemon shake-ups! Honestly, it's one of the most fun outdoor activity centers in Central Illinois.

919 N Swords Ave., 309-676-3628
kartville.com

FIND 400 ACRES TO EXPLORE
AT THREE SISTERS PARK

Three Sisters Park is a 400-acre private park, just a 15-minute drive north of Peoria, near the Illinois River. Besides being the venue for the famous Summer Camp Music Festival, the park provides year-round events and entertainment. Each spring, grade-schoolers get the opportunity to experience some hands-on education on how agriculture was done in 1918. Interactive demonstrations will teach them about soil, planting, and equipment. In the fall they host Spider Hill Haunted Attractions each Friday and Saturday in October, where you can see the Massacre Mansion, Trail of Terror, and the Zombie Invasion. The Trail of Terror takes people through the haunted forest and zombie invasion. You can find craft and vendor fairs, see border collies show off their skills with the sheep, and even play in a poker tournament. You can visit the 1918 farmhouse, barn, and windmill, and see a show at the outdoor amphitheater as well.

17189 N State St., Rte. 29, Chillicothe, 309-274-8837
threesisterspark.com

COME WAVE TO SANTA
AT PEORIA'S SANTA CLAUS PARADE, RUNNING FOR 135 YEARS!

Held each year the Friday after Thanksgiving, it began as a competition between downtown department stores Schipper & Block and Harned, Berner & Von Maur to promote shopping where the "real Santa" was. One year, Schipper & Block brought Santa Claus into town on a train on Water Street. As the years went on, thousands of people would flock and watch the parade participants, and the event grew each season. Enjoy the classic costumed characters, antique cars, dancers, cheerleading teams, and especially the school bands playing Christmas classics and all the Christmas floats going by. Bring a bag for candy, because your kids will have no problem filling it up with goodies! Wait with anticipation to wave to Santa Claus, who always brings the parade to a close. It's always cold in Peoria, Illinois, this time of year, so dress warm, and enjoy making lifetime memories downtown.

Search the City of Peoria, Illinois, website
for more information and time/location. peoriagov.org

TIP
Peoria also hosts a pretty darned good St. Patrick's Day Parade each year downtown.

JOIN US IN JULY
FOR THE HEART OF ILLINOIS FAIR

Head on over to Peoria Expo Gardens for the Heart of Illinois Fair. In this showcase of the Midwest's agricultural history, you can see tractor pulls and livestock, and visit the petting zoo. There are classic carnival rides, games to win some prizes, car shows, and of course delicious food and drinks. Elephant ears and lemonade shake-ups are a must! Some years they host a Demolition Derby, and there are concerts for the adults to enjoy. One really exciting addition is the Heart of Illinois's Got Talent Competition! Contestants go through an extremely vigorous judging competition to the finals, with first, second, and third prizes receiving financial prizes. People with talents in music, comedy, theater, and magic bring a large crowd to cheer them on. So, if you are heading to Peoria in July, don't forget to plan a night or afternoon at the fair.

heartofillinoisfair.com

OTHER FESTIVALS

Chillicothe Days Carnival, held in June each year
Washington Good Neighbor Days
Elmwood Strawberry Festival
Canton Art on Main
Tremont Turkey Festival
Italian American Festa
Pekin Marigold Festival
Morton Pumpkin Festival

DO A STAND-UP COMEDY ROUTINE
AT THE JUKEBOX COMEDY CLUB

Do your friends tell you that you should be a comedian? Visit Open Mic Comedy Nights at the Jukebox Comedy Club and show them what you've got. They ask that you have at least five minutes of material prepared, but it costs nothing but your ego, potentially! The Jukebox Comedy Club often has currently popular comedians, and being so close to Chicago, some up-and-coming funny guys and gals from Chicago and other cities entertain us by practicing their jokes out in Peoria. Enjoy some food and drinks at the bar. It is best to purchase tickets online ahead of time to see your favorite comedians. Staff is friendly, and it's the oldest-running comedy club in Central Illinois, opening in 1990. It is open Wednesday and Thursday from 7 p.m. to midnight, and on Friday and Saturday from 7 p.m. to 1 a.m. This venue is for adults over age 21 only.

3527 W Farmington Rd., 309-635-3900
jukeboxcomedy.com

LACE YOUR SKATES YEAR-ROUND
AT OWENS CENTER

Grab the kids and go to Owens Center, an indoor skating center that has two National Hockey League-size ice-skating rinks. Ice-skating is a great way to get some fun and different kinds of exercise. Even for the not-so-good skaters, families can have fun trying a new activity together and laugh while Dad falls on his bum, or big sister holds onto Mom for dear life. There are public skate times, and ice skate rentals available. Kids can get year ice-skating lessons in different sessions year-round, and they offer hockey and figure-skating programs as well. A course offering pre-hockey skills partners with the Peoria Youth Hockey Association, with house and travel leagues. You can host a private rental there, and it has a snack shop, as well as yearly special events like Skate with Santa!

1019 W Lake Ave., 309-686-3368
peoriaparks.org/places/owens-center

PICK YOUR APPLES RIGHT OFF THE TREES
AT TANNERS ORCHARD

Established in 1947 by the Tanner family, Tanners Orchard is a few miles north of Peoria and has over 11,000 apple trees, with 17 different varieties of apples to choose from. Take a ride in the covered wagon in September on festival days, and pick your apples right off of the tree and your pumpkins from the pumpkin patch. Kiddos won't want to miss the fun at the Back 40 Fun Acres, with a wonderful playground featuring dozens of attractions. On festival days, look for pony rides, a barrel train, face painting, Grain Train, Jumping Jack pad, giant bubbles, swing, and more. There is a large corn maze, sunflower field, and lots of farm animals: bunnies, goats, llamas, horses, and chickens. There is a bakery and daily lunch and dinner specials, and do not leave without purchasing the best apple cider and apple cider donuts in Central Illinois.

740 State Ste. 40, Speer, 309-228-9156
tannersorchard.com

OTHER ORCHARDS

Ackerman Family Farms
Arends Orchard
Christ Orchard
Orchard Hill Farm & Country Store
Partridge Point Orchard
Pleasant Row
Roth Pumpkin Patch

RUN, WALK, AND CYCLE
ON THE ROCK ISLAND TRAIL

The trail is an old Rock Island Railroad Company railroad line from Peoria to Rock Island, on which the first train passed through in 1871. It had both passenger and freight trains traveling through, until traffic slowed in the late 1950s. The former railroad was turned into a tree-lined walking, running, and biking trail decades later. It is surrounded by beautiful trees, creeks, and prairies. Starting in the mid-1960s, the Forest Park Foundation acquired the abandoned Rock Island & Peoria Railroad from Alta to Toulon. The land was transferred to the State of Illinois, and it opened for use as a public trail in 1989. It runs through Peoria Heights, not too far from Grand Drive, has an arched bridge over Knoxville at Junction City, and continues through at the Kellar Branch, North Peoria, Alta, and north through Dunlap, up to Toulon, Illinois. There is a parking lot, restroom facilities, and drinking fountains at the Alta section.

Rock Island Trail at Alta Road Trailhead
traillink.com/trail/rock-island-trail

SIDE TRIPS, IF YOU ARE INTERESTED IN LOCAL RAILROAD HISTORY
Galesburg Railroad Museum
211 S Seminary St., Galesburg, 309-342-9400
galesburgrailroadmuseum.org

Chillicothe Historical
Society House Museum
723 N 4th St., Chillicothe

Rock Island Railroad Depot Museum
227 W Cedar St., Chillicothe
chillicothehistorical.org

WITNESS WINTER WONDERLAND AND DRIVE-THROUGH LIGHTS
AT THE EAST PEORIA FESTIVAL OF LIGHTS

Fireworks kick off the Festival of Lights, which begins with the Parade of Lights on a Saturday near Thanksgiving week each year, a traditional two-mile-long parade with folks lined up in East Peoria. It's followed with Folepi's Winter Wonderland as a drive-through Christmas light display. This is an award-winning, 2020 Heavyweights Division Winner on ABC's *The Great Christmas Light Fight*. There are dreamy, horse-drawn carriage rides that take you to Folepi's Gift Shop and the historic Four Corners, and through the Winter Wonderland of lights. The lights stay up following the traditional parade until just after the New Year, in early January. Runners can partake in the Folepi River Trail Classic four-mile run that brings in runners from all over the country! There are even more events such as Breakfast and Photos with Santa, and the "Get Lit" New Year Eve's celebration, which offers family-friendly activities.

855-833-5327
cityofeastpeoria.com

TIPS

Grab a burger at the Burger Barge while you're on that side of the river!

1401 N Main St., East Peoria, 309-694-9191

If you loved the Burger Barge, you can travel a little further to Kuchie's on the Water and get the Original Shipwreck Bloody Mary, which won the title of best Bloody Mary in Peoria several years in a row! Shipwreck Bloody Mary is layered a half-foot above the glass with pickles, cheeses, meats, and more!

597 Wesley Rd., Creve Coeur, 309-427-3000

CELEBRATE IRISH CULTURE
AT THE PEORIA IRISH FEST

The Peoria Irish Fest is one of the biggest Irish festivals in the entire Midwest. It is a three-day festival, held in August every year. There are Irish cultural and village displays, Irish food, and four stages of Irish bands, and the goal is to feature a band or two from Ireland each year. The Peoria Irish Fest brings in around 10,000 visitors, and each festival will have around a dozen bands over the three days. Bring the family to view and root on the ancient "highland games" on the grassy field. Enjoy excellent dancers from Flynn's School of Irish Dance and watch them do an Irish jig or an Irish reel, and even some classic hard-shoe. There are lots of kids' activities, and tons of vendors selling Irish wares, art, and other goods. Don't forget the Irish beer and whiskey! Churchgoers can partake in a Sunday morning Irish Mass at St. Mary's Cathedral at 10:30 a.m.

Peoria RiverFront Events/CEFCU Center Stage @ The Landing
200 NE Water St.
peoriairishfest.com

TIP
Visit St. Mary's Cathedral while you are in town. A historic downtown treasure, this cathedral was completed in 1889, and you will notice the beauty of the stone: It is Anamosa limestone, and there are two beautiful spires that can be seen from across the river. It is filled with precious art, brightly colored stained glass windows, and a majestic pipe organ that has over 3,000 pipes. The famous Mother Teresa, now Saint Teresa of Calcutta, visited in 1995. 607 NE Madison Ave., 309-673-6317, catholicpeoria.com

WILLKOMMEN
TO PEORIA OKTOBERFEST

Together, the Peoria Park District and the German-American Central Society bring this wonderful event to Peoria every year. Enjoy learning about and hearing German drinking songs, and see folks dressed up in lederhosen, the traditional shorts with suspenders, or the dirndl, which is the dress with short sleeves and gathered skirt. Drink German beer from a stein! Oktoberfest is held in September at Peoria RiverFront Events/CEFCU Center Stage @ The Landing.

The original Oktoberfest was held in 1810 in honor of a Bavarian crown prince. Peoria Oktoberfest starts on Friday night and is a three-day festival. There is a large tent and picnic tables, and you can celebrate German heritage with German music, a log-sawing contest, and the Lindenhof Echoes Alphenhorns. Runners, don't miss the Das Bier Run 5k. German attire is welcome. Find traditional German food and beer, and consider joining the men's and women's Bier Stein Holding Contest.

309-682-1200
oktoberfestpeoria.com

TIP

Get a delicious German dinner on Friday nights and celebrate German culture at events year-round at the Lindenhof of Peoria German Restaurant! 7601 N Harker Dr., peoriagermans.net

CELEBRATE PEORIA'S JUNETEENTH FEST
AT JOHN GWYNN PARK

Peoria hosts the Juneteenth Celebration, which recognizes the date of June 19th, 1865, the date that slavery finally ended in all of the United States, which came two years after President Abraham Lincoln spoke and signed the famous Emancipation Proclamation. Juneteenth commemorates the day when the last Black slaves were finally told of their freedom: In Texas, there were still over a quarter of a million souls still enslaved until two months after the end of the Civil War, and on June 19th, 1865, Union soldiers came to Galveston, Texas, to deliver the news finally that all African Americans were free. It was declared a state holiday in Illinois and signed into law. There is a live DJ and music and dance performances. You also can enjoy guest speakers giving meaningful presentations. Food and drink and vendors will sell goods, local officials will be on hand, and you can learn more about the community at information booths.

The event is held at Carver Center, John Gwynn Park.

HEAR
THE HERITAGE ENSEMBLE

Heritage Ensemble is a chorale group that uses our heritage to bring beautiful music to the community and use their musical talents to build a bridge between all people. The Heritage Ensemble sings African American music and performs gospel, ragtime, jazz, blues, and more traditional African American work songs. Their mission is to make the Peoria area a better place to live together. It is a not-for-profit arts organization. One of their awesome annual events is its annual Dr. Martin Luther King Jr. Choral Celebration. This event takes place each year in January, at the ICC Performing Arts Center Main Stage Theatre, East Peoria Campus. The group formed in 1999, has performed a concert annually since 2000 to recognize the Juneteenth Celebration, and together with the city of Peoria was key in celebrating this event, now an Illinois State Holiday. Heritage Ensemble hosts an annual jazz fundraiser concert every year in November.

309-691-2000
heritageensemble.com

TIP

Visit the African American Hall of Fame Museum, a small but meaningful museum housed in the historic Proctor Recreation Center. It hosts art, history, and exhibits teaching others about the achievements of African American contributors to culture, society, and politics. 309 S Dusable St., aahfmpeoria.org

ATTEND THE CHRYSANTHEMUM SHOW
AT LUTHY BOTANICAL GARDEN

Situated on over five acres, this botanical showcase includes a combination of over 12 gardens, including a Tropical Conservatory! Happen to be in Peoria during the holiday season? Do not miss the annual holiday Poinsettia Show, held inside the Conservatory with tons of tropical plants, flowers, and hundreds of poinsettias. Stroll along one of the Candlelight Walks with your sweetie, and embrace the live holiday music and romance. The annual Chrysanthemum Show takes place in the fall and highlights brilliant mums and pumpkins. The annual Lily Show takes place each spring, and combines the beauty of the tropical plants with spring flowers/ plants and, of course, lilies! This is a wonderful way to celebrate the warmth and growth of spring. There is the annual Mother's Day Orchid Show you won't want to miss either. There are numerous themed outdoor gardens, and water features as well. The gardens are open daily at 10 a.m. and close at 4:30 p.m.

2520 N Prospect Rd., 309-681-3506
peoriaparks.org/luthy-botanical-garden

TIP

Illinois Central College Arboretum is another beautiful botanical garden. Horticulture Department, 1 College Dr., East Peoria, 309-694-8446 icc.edu/arts

SEE THE VALLEY
ON THE BRIDGE-TO-BRIDGE RIVER DRIVE

The Peoria Heights Arts Collaborative's Bridge-to-Bridge River Drive connects five towns along the Illinois River, and showcases the best of what each town has to offer. The communities of Peoria Heights, Chillicothe, Lacon, Henry, and Spring Bay take part each fall. You can take an airplane ride in Lacon and fly overhead, seeing the Illinois River Valley from a bird's-eye view. There are vendors, food, arts and crafts, events in each town, craft vendors at Shore Acres Park in Chillicothe, and live music, crafts, and shopping at Historic Downtown Second Street in Chillicothe. Activities have included a mural painting in downtown Lacon, and arts and festivities in Peoria Heights and Henry. Go fishing, see the beautiful Spring Bay for a boat show, or be part of a fishing tournament. Henry will have vendors and a cruise-in. There is a fashion show in Peoria Heights, tons of food from the farmers market, and live music. Enjoy a weekend celebration of these amazing small towns near the Illinois River.

320-616-1640
peoriaheightsarts.com/bridge-to-bridge

WALK THROUGH THOUSANDS OF GIANT SUNFLOWERS
AT JUBILEE STATE PARK AND STAY TO PLAY

Each summer, Jubilee State Park plants sunflowers that bloom by the thousands in fields at the park. You will have to check the website to find out exactly when the best blooms have arrived, as they only last for a few weeks, shining brightly in their glory in the sunshine. Photographers and families come from all over the state to this park, in Brimfield, Illinois. Jubilee offers over 3,200 acres of land and woods and fields to explore. It's on the National Register of Historic Places and is run by the Illinois Department of Natural Resources. There are hiking trails, camping sites, cross-country skiing, mountain bike trails, horseback-riding trail areas, fishing, some hunting with preregistration, picnicking, and more. The land is beautiful, and there are many animals to see, including 160 species of birds for the birdwatchers. Scenic Jubilee Creek runs through the park, and is a tributary of the Kickapoo Creek.

13921 W Rte. 150, Brimfield, 309-446-3758
www2.illinois.gov/dnr/parks/pages/jubileecollege.aspx

TIP

Visit the tiniest pioneer church, St. Mary of Lourdes, on the way to Jubilee State Park in Brimfield at St. Patrick's Cemetery. It is so tiny! The Catholic Church hosts a few masses a year. It is the oldest church in the Peoria diocese. Eat some pie at the nearby Jubilee Cafe!

PARTY LIKE A ROCK STAR
AT CRUSENS BAR

Crusens opened in the mid-1980s on War Memorial Drive in Peoria. The Crusen boys created a fantastic establishment to bring in live music weekly, and grew through the years. Three locations operate now: War Memorial, Farmington Road by Bradley Park and near Bradley University, and on Route 29 in Creve Coeur. They offer live music, and draw a huge crowd, at all three of the festive establishments. Order the delicious tenderloin, or the award-winning wings in a variety of flavors. There is a specialty dish called Chicken Don with Mimi Sauce. Don't forget the delicious, thin-crust pizza: Spice it up with the Crusens six cheese pizza and homemade pizza sauce. There are tons of sandwiches and burgers, a kids' menu, and specially priced lunch menu. There's plenty to enjoy, whether lunch or dinner, or partying your heart out at night to rock and roll or a hot country band!

2117 W Farmington Rd., West Peoria
426 E War Memorial Dr.
1007 N Main St., Creve Coeur
crusenspeoria.com

TIP

Keep up-to-date with the Peoria music scene with Peoria Music Live! This website shares info on when and where to find your favorite bands and awesome music venues to try. peoriamusiclive.com

FOR THOSE WHO LIKE TO PARTY HEARTY: FARMINGTON ROAD BARS/RESTAURANTS

Shelton's Bar
2016 W Farmington Rd., West Peoria, 309-981-5635
facebook.com/sheltonsbar

Country Club BBQ
2510 W Farmington Rd., West Peoria, 309-966-3766
bbqpeoria.com/index.html

Jimmy's Bar
2801 W Farmington Rd., West Peoria, 309-676-4021
facebook.com/jimmysbarwestpeoria

The Trolley
2411 W Farmington Rd., West Peoria, 309-637-4722
facebook.com/thetrolley1932

SEE
THE SCOTTISH RITE THEATRE

The Scottish Rite Theatre was built almost a century ago, in Gothic Cathedral style, and has undergone a multimillion-dollar, multi-year renovation, keeping much of the original features of the historic venue. Referred to as the "second life" of the theater, the renovation prompted many discoveries, including a hidden orchestra pit, original light fixtures sitting in a corner in crumpled-up boxes, and gorgeous original woodwork that had been painted and was painstakingly stripped and restained throughout the entire building. Everything from the breathtaking ceiling to the stained glass windows and tuckpointing outside was refurbished, the bathrooms were made handicapped-accessible, and no details were missed. It is now a performance venue, a destination for everyone from local arts groups to national and regional touring theatrical groups, and musicians from all over the world! There is even a ballroom on the lower level.

400 NE Perry Ave., 309-324-8587
scottishritepeoria.com

FIND FAMILY FUN
AT THE PEORIA RIVERFRONT MUSEUM

The Peoria Riverfront Museum (PRM) opened in 2012 and is located in downtown Peoria, overlooking the Illinois riverfront. People can learn about art, science, history, and more. PRM is an American Alliance of Museums-accredited, Smithsonian-affiliated nonprofit museum. Patrons can visit traveling major exhibitions and learn about Peoria as well. Watch the stars and planets in the Dome Planetarium, or watch a movie on the Giant Screen Theater, a 52-by-70-foot screen. There are extensive collections of art and science, some of which are permanent, and others that rotate out. There is a section dedicated to teaching about the ecology of the Illinois River, as well as the history and industry of the Illinois River. The local history section teaches you about Peoria's past, from thousands of years back to modern times, and highlights different businesses, industries, and influential people who have charted Peoria's history. The PRM hosts international traveling exhibits from places like the American Museum of Natural History in New York.

309-686-7000
riverfrontmuseum.org

OTHER MUSEUMS/EXHIBITS

Peoria Holocaust Memorial
Button Project
Washington and Liberty Streets,
on the grounds of the Peoria
Riverfront Museum

Caterpillar Visitors Center & Museum
110 SW Washington St.
309-675-0606
caterpillar.com/en/company/
visitors-center.html

● ●

Wildlife Prairie Park
Photo courtesy of Mark Monge

SPORTS
AND RECREATION

POPULATE DOZER PARK
WITH THE PEORIA CHIEFS

Peoria has a truly rich history with baseball, going back to the late 1800s. There were historic Peoria teams named the Peoria Reds, the Distillers, and the Peoria Tractors in the 1800s and early 1900s. After several more name changes, Pete Vonachen bought the Peoria Suns in the 1980s, and then later changed it to the Peoria Chiefs. Dozer Park opened in 2002, and the name "Dozers" is a tribute to the Peoria connection with Caterpillar's bulldozers. It is a top-of-the-line baseball stadium, with stadium seating, special box seats, and an awesome green, grassy field for general admission. Thousands of people attend Chiefs games in the stadium, located near the Warehouse District, and is a few blocks away from the river. It's fun for the entire family. The Peoria Chiefs are a Class A minor league team, and have had an affiliation for two decades as a Saint Louis Cardinals Advanced A Affiliate.

Stadium, arena, and sports venue sports club
309-680-4000
peoria.chiefs.milb.com/index.jsp?sid=t443

TIP
Check out the Louisville Slugger Sports Complex while you are here! It is a top-of-the-line indoor and outdoor stadium, arena, and sports venue. 8400 N Orange Prairie Rd., sluggerpeoria.com

VISIT WILDLIFE PRAIRIE PARK,
JEWEL OF THE MIDWEST

Wildlife Prairie Park is a 2,000-acre zoological park with over 150 animals and 50 different species native to Illinois that both children and adults alike can enjoy for an entire day in nature. This "Gem of the Midwest" is a conservation, education, and recreation nonprofit organization, with some of the most beautiful scenic views and landscapes anywhere in the country. Visitors from all over the world come to enjoy observing the animals in their natural habitats in open-air environments, including bison, waterfowl, black bear, and more. It has opportunities for all walks of life and energy levels. You can stroll leisurely along the trails, and ring the school bell at the authentic, old-fashioned schoolhouse, go inside a prairie log cabin and prairie garden, and view farm animals. You can wake up to view the bison outside of your cabin. There are also cross-country bike trails, disc golf, fishing, and canoeing.

3826 N Taylor Rd., Hanna City
wildlifeprairiepark.org

PERUSE AN AWARD-WINNING DISTILLERY
IN THE HISTORIC WAREHOUSE DISTRICT

Peoria, Illinois once held the claim as the Whiskey Capital of the world from the 1800s up to Prohibition. There were once dozens of distilleries in what was called "Whiskey Row" in the now Historic Warehouse District, where the BLACK BAND Distillery is located at 1000 Southwest Adams Street. They host the bragging rights of being a "certified organic craft distillery," with the farm to table philosophy that helps bring the authenticity of their award winning spirits to their restaurant and bar using locally sourced food, and grains for the alcohol from Illinois farmers. They won six medals at the San Francisco World Spirits Competition, winning several Silver medals, Gin that won Gold, and Double Gold medals with the Bourbon and Coffee Liqueur. Don't leave Peoria without booking a tour of this distillery, and learn all about the distilling process, and taste some delicious samples as well.

blackband-distillery.com

TIP
JK Williams Distilling is another award winning distillery and is part of a growing trend of bringing Peoria's history with distilling whiskey back to life. 8635 N Industrial Rd., 617-755-5206, jkwilliamsdistilling.com

RUN THE STEAMBOAT PEORIA
AND RACE THROUGH HISTORIC PARTS OF THE CITY

People from all over the world sign up to run the Steamboat Peoria, known as the "world's fastest four miles." Consisting of a one-mile, four-mile, and 15k race, it is held in June each year, beginning and ending at Peoria's riverfront. Good news, you can run or walk this course! Cost is $40 for early registrants, and increases in price to $50 closer to the event. The four-mile race kicks off at 7 a.m. and is a very fast, smooth course. This race has taken place for 48 years, brings in thousands of men and women each year, and requires hundreds of volunteers to organize. Peoria's history and connection to steamboats is an integral part of its story, connecting the resources and people in Peoria with business and trade up to Chicago, and down to St. Louis. The steamboats left their legacy in Peoria.

steamboatclassic.org

TAKE A 16.4 MILE HLC RIVER JAUNT
ALONG THE ILLINOIS RIVER, HOSTED BY THE CHILLICOTHE CHAMBER OF COMMERCE

Canoers and kayakers from all over the Midwest bring their canoes/kayaks and participate in the annual scenic, 16.4 mile, HLC River Jaunt (Henry, Lacon, and Chillicothe) held in August. For $50 they get a T-shirt and decal commemorating the event. The jaunt begins in Henry Harbor, continues on to Lacon Marina, and lands at the beautiful Shore Acres Park in Chillicothe. Participants are provided with a light snack, boxed lunch in Lacon, and a hot, home-cooked dinner with all the fixings at the finish. The sight of 100 various colors and styles of canoes and kayaks taking off is a mesmerizing sight to see. The beautiful waters and wildlife along the way is not to be missed. See eagles, herons, cranes, and, of course, the crazy, flying and slapping Asian carp! The Henry, Lacon-Sparland, and Chillicothe Community fire protection districts all help to ensure a fun and safe event.

309-274-4556, 309-857-6844
chillicothechamber.com

MORE FUN THINGS TO DO IN CHILLICOTHE

Swim at **Shore Acres Park and Pool** and go
down the waterslides!
100 Park Blvd., Chillicothe
chillicotheparkdistrict.org

Hike the trails at **Coal Hollow Park**
chillicotheparkdistrict.org/facility/coal-hollow-park

Purchase a Family Day Pass at **Pearce Community
Center** and play and swim indoors on a cold or rainy day!
309-274-4209
pearcecc.com

HAVE A PAINTBALL BATTLE
AT CHILLICOTHE PAINTBALL PITS

The adventurer's fantasy playground on over 40 acres of land, affectionately known as "the pits," has over 22 forts on eight playing fields. Bring the kids and challenge them to a battle! Some of the specials are the speedball field, the village field, the castle, the Western Town, and more. Hide from your opponents and gain the upper hand, attacking them with paintball pellets. You will have to sign a liability waiver, and you pay fees to rent the paintball gun, face mask, field fee, and paintball pellets. There are referees who help keep the fighting fair. There are a variety of packages to choose from, from 200 rounds of paintball pellets, up to 2,000 rounds of paintball pellets. It's available to rent for any kind of party, and there are a few grills on-site.

21324 N Benedict St., Chillicothe, 309-274-5251

TRY "GLAMPING"
AT SANKOTY LAKES RESORT

Go "glamping," swimming, relaxing, and dining at Sankoty Lakes Resort. Sankoty is a world-class resort located just 15 minutes away from Peoria on the Sankoty Aquifer, in Spring Bay, Illinois. There is a beautiful series of cabins, heated glamping tents, a beautiful RV park, and tons of activities including sunbathing, swimming, marshmallow roasting, sitting around the campfire, dancing, and relaxing under moonlit starry nights. Folks can also do fly fishing on a catch-and-release basis, go on a hike, go biking, go birdwatching and view majestic bald eagles, swim, and kayak or canoe. Hungry? Enjoy a restaurant called The Woolly Bugger that serves a locally sourced menu in indoor and outdoor dining, with gorgeous views of the lake. There is also The 1840 Ranch you can rent for a private, peaceful time. Experience the best that the Midwest has to offer!

sankotylakes.com
the1840ranch.com
thewoollybuggersankoty.com

TIP

If you enjoyed Sankoty Lake Resort, you will also enjoy drinks, dining, and entertainment inside and in open air at Betty Jayne Center for Performing Arts, a unique live music venue, named after the developer Kim Blickenstaff's mother, who was an actress/performer in the vaudeville days. 1327 E Kelly Ave., Peoria Heights, 309-570-1532 thebettyjayne.com

---

MOTORCYCLISTS UNITE
IN THE PEORIA MOTORCYCLE CLUB

The Peoria Motorcycle Club (PMC), founded in 1931, is a family-friendly club open to men, women, and children, and is the home of the world's longest consecutively running dirt track race! PMC was started by brothers Bruce and Bob Walters, who happened to own the Peoria area's Harley Davidson Motorcycle dealership, which is still operating today! People from all over the world have traveled to Peoria to attend races at PMC, and they have hosted the Grand National Race since 1947. PMC has also hosted the National Championship Tourist Trophy races since then. PMC track is unlike any dirt track for motorcycles in the country, as it is a five-eighths-mile, clay track, and is a jump followed by a righthand turn. Motorcycle riders come from all over the United States. These and other annual races at PMC bring in between 4,000 to 8,000 motorcycle racing fans each year.

605 Cameron Ln., Bartonville, 309-697-4981
peoriamotorcycleclub.net

TIP

Go see the races at historic Peoria Speedway. Five divisions race each weekend, including Street Stocks and Modifieds. General admission is for ages 11 and up, children 10 and under free. Pit passes can be purchased as well. Carnival rides and vendors have been added to some of the weekend events! 3520 W Farmington Rd., 309-510-3145 peoriaspeedway.com

---

WELCOME TO THE FARM: HAVE INTERACTIVE FUN
AT FON DU LAC FARM PARK

Step back in time when you take your family to Fon du Lac Farm Park, which is inspired by a farm from the 1920s. There is a lovely scene as you enter and see the large pond with the ducks, which children can feed with food purchased on-site. Part of the pond is like a babbling brook, and it just adds to the nostalgia. There are chickens, pigs, bunnies, goats, cows, ponies, and a horse for the children to meet and feed as well. They can do the activities in the barn and slide down the slides, see the one-room schoolhouse and home museum that make learning about rural life from the past poignant, and make lifelong memories. There is a large playground on-site. The farm allows you to bring in your own picnic lunch and drinks so you can bring the entire family for the day to this amazing petting zoo/park.

305 Neumann Dr., East Peoria, 309-694-2195
fondulacpark.com

TIP

Visit Clover Haven Healing Ranch, a small therapy ranch that allows people who have suffered from trauma, abuse, or mental health issues to interact with the animals. Please set up an appointment with the owners ahead of time by messaging on their Facebook page. E Cloverdale Rd., Chillicothe

KEEP THE BIG WHEELS TURNING
AT WHEELS O' TIME MUSEUM

Wheels O' Time Museum has six large structures filled with all things wheels! It opened in 1977 and has grown each year since, with exhibitions and interactive activities for kids and grownups to enjoy. Wheels is open six months a year, with its season running from May 1 to October 31, Wednesdays through Sundays from noon to 5 p.m. The main building has antique/classic cars and a clock room, electric motors, steam engines, and a River to Rails Exhibit. There is a Ford Building that has cars and tractors; a new exhibit that has an antique airplane, military vehicles, and a Peoria history section; and a Farm Building with vintage farm tools, equipment, vintage machinery, and antique fire truck. There are exhibits outside as well, including real railroad train cars: a Rock Island steam locomotive, Milwaukee Road Combine Car, TP & W Caboose, Pullman railroad cars, and also the 1938 LeTourneau Steel House, with the Central Illinois Landmarks Foundation, Peoria Historical Society.

1710 W Woodside Dr., Dunlap, 309-243-9020
wheelsotime.org

FIND BEAUTIFUL HIDDEN GEMS
IN SOMMER FARM PARK, PART OF THE PEORIA PARK DISTRICT

There are opportunities to see history come to life at the 320-acre Sommer Farm Park, with multiple events and sites showcasing its heritage. There is the Koerner Homestead, which is now used as offices, and an 1800s wooden schoolhouse that serves a dual purpose as a wedding chapel. There is even a tiny, ancient cemetery that belonged to the original family owners of the farm park! A pioneer homestead from 1855, the park includes a pond, some farm animals, a beautiful Sommer North Trail and a woodland trail. A "living history" exhibit teaches about life as a pioneer during the 1850s. Visitors can see blacksmithing, candle making, and other fun things like horse and cart rides. Civil War and World War II reenactments take place each year and are very popular. Check out Ancient Oaks Day Camp, bringing kids together with animals and agriculture. Campers will also enjoy some fishing, canoeing, and make campfires.

6329 N Koerner Rd., Edwards, 309-691-8423
peoriaparks.org/venue/sommer-farm

CELEBRATE THE WOODLANDS
AT FOREST PARK NATURE CENTER

One of the most beautiful places in the Peoria Park District, and also part of the Illinois State Nature Reserve, the center hosts over 500 acres of walking/hiking trails, beautiful mature forestry, and scenic hills and streams, as well as simpler, flat trails to walk. No matter the season, you can find nature at its finest here, with a beautiful tree canopy along the trail while you hike to the forest, and the breathtaking fall colors each autumn. Check out the Nature Center A-frame building and Trailhead Nature Store, an educational history museum that teaches about local animals and plants and trees. Kiddos will see the wild turkeys, native birds, and other wildlife, including an abundance of elegant deer throughout the reserve. Special events are open to the public, including the Earth Day Festival, reptile education when the Central Illinois Herpetological Society meets monthly, and meetings of the Heart of Illinois Sierra Club and Peoria Audubon Society. Pack a picnic lunch!

5809 N Forest Park Dr., Peoria Heights, 309-686-3360
peoriaparks.org/forest-park-nature-center

SING IN THE WOODS AT TAWNY OAKS FIELD STATION
AT SINGING WOODS NATURE RESERVE

In the mood for a quick hike? Tawny Oaks Field Station has a flat, handicapped-accessible, half-mile Prairie Trail in a giant loop, with fields of wildflowers and native flowers on both sides of the path. Find informational signs around the loop that share information about the native animals and insects. In the warmer months, watch an occasional snake sunbathing on the ground, bumblebees buzzing from wildflower to wildflower, bright, beautiful butterflies and dragonflies flying at ease all around the milkweed, and frogs singing in the seasonal, ephemeral pond along the way. There's a pavilion, and a visitors' center that's open seasonally, with several wooded hiking trails on over 700 acres and five miles of trails in the woods, with some flowing creeks. Some paths go uphill, but trails are clear and pretty easy to navigate. Special events include the Native Plant Sale and Stars Over Peoria, which is a guided walk with a naturalist.

715 W Singing Woods Rd., Edelstein, 309-418-7051
peoriaparks.org/tawny-oaks

RELAX
AT HISTORIC CAMP WOKANDA

Historic Camp Wokanda, founded originally as a Boy Scout camp in 1937, offers year-round camping, events, and rental use. There are 316 acres of woods and a lake for canoeing and fishing! In the warmer seasons, you can call the Peoria Park District and rent a canoe to take out on the lake to canoe and fish. There are overnight rentals for cabins and the Historic OA Lodge and Dining Hall. You can pitch a tent and camp also. Groups or families can go on guided nature tours; it is the perfect place for family reunions or corporate team-building events. Visiting in the wintertime? They host a "Chill Billy!" winter sporting event that includes everything from ice fishing and winter trail running to a winter birding hike. There is also a Maple Sap Harvest, using old-fashioned methods of tapping a tree to make maple syrup, and people can also purchase "Camp Wokanda Maple Syrup" for sale.

620 E Boy Scout Rd., Chillicothe, 309-579-2157
peoriaparks.org/camp-wokanda

FOLLOW THE YELLOW BRICK ROAD
AT THE ILLINOIS OZ FEST

Illinois Oz Fest is held once a year in August at Butler Haynes Park in Mapleton, Illinois, minutes away from Peoria. Children of all ages and the young at heart dress up as their favorite characters from the beloved movie, *The Wizard of Oz*. Kids will enjoy magic shows, puppet shows, and bouncy houses. "The Spirit of Oz," a professional premier troupe of Wizard of Oz characters Dorothy, the Scarecrow, the Tin Man, the Lion, Toto, and more, will be on hand to chat with and take photographs. Take a hayrack ride with Auntie Em telling stories, and enjoy concessions, vendors, and crafts. The festival is only one day, running from 9 a.m. to 6 p.m., but is jam-packed with activities from start to finish, including the Spirit of Oz troupe character show, the Dorothy Parade. The festival features a real "yellow brick road" and festively bright "Munchkin Garden" of beautiful flowers. People come from all over the state to attend this magical festival.

Hollis Park District Parks and Recreational Services
9424 S Mapleton Rd., Mapleton, 309-697-2944
hollispark.org/oz-fest

FIND A WATERFALL AND SANDSTONE FORMATIONS
AT ROCKY GLEN PARK

Rocky Glen is a smaller, but gorgeous, park, part of the Peoria Park District, that has beautiful rock formations, a scenic, 200-foot hill, winding creek, and a waterfall. There's a two-mile hiking loop near Kickapoo Creek and the railroad tracks. You can see the geology as it features partially moss-covered sandstone formations, and has large coal deposits. Spy an old mine shaft and see evidence of the coal industry from the past. There is a group called "Friends of Rocky Glen" that helps host many events each year and sponsors group hikes, native plant sales, trash cleanups, and a newer annual event called the Kickapoo Creek Festival. The Friends were instrumental in getting consideration with the Peoria Park District for a small parking lot and trail markers on the hiking loop. There are no restrooms or picnic tables.

309-573-2354
friendsofrockyglen.org

TIP

If you loved Rocky Glen Park, consider taking
a guided tour with "Friends of Rocky Glen"
and "Friends of Horseshoe Bottoms," volunteers
working to help convert a 200-acre area of farm fields
and woods along Kickapoo Creek for restoration to
protect wildlife and biodiversity.

Kickapoo Creek Watershed Conservation
and Natural Area

CANOE, FISH, OR BIRDWATCH
AT THE BANNER MARSH STATE FISH AND WILDLIFE AREA

Want to coast on a boat among the American lotus flowers floating atop the natural waters? You can find them at the Banner Marsh, a 4,363-acre, freshwater marsh connecting 200 water entities together with grasslands. These lands used to be farmlands and were previously used for coal mining, when the Illinois Department of Natural Resources bought these lands that border on the Illinois River. This is a paradise for nature lovers: You can see beautiful great blue herons, American white pelicans, Canada geese, and white swans, or spend the day fishing, pack a picnic lunch in your canoe, do dog training, or even hunt at certain times of the year. The Banner Marsh is perfect for amateur and professional photographers. There are boat ramps, restrooms, and picnic areas. No boat fishing is allowed during waterfowl hunting season; however, you can still go fishing on the banks during certain hours during this time.

309-647-9184
www2.illinois.gov/dnr/Parks/Pages/BannerMarsh.aspx

TIPS

While visiting Peoria, it is definitely worth your time to travel about an hour north to the historic **Starved Rock State Park** and take in some of the most spectacular views in the entire Midwest. Stay overnight at **Starved Rock State Lodge & Conference Center**, and dining in the restaurant. The lodge was built in the 1930s, and is glorious!
1 Lodge Ln., Oglesby, 815-667-4211
starvedrocklodge.com

Take a shorter visit just 15 minutes from Peoria to **Fort Creve Coeur**, which is a replica of the original fort from 1680, located on the Illinois River.
stateparks.com/fort_creve_coeur_state_park_in_illinois.html

INDULGE YOUR SENSES
AT EMIQUON NATIONAL WILDLIFE REFUGE

Emiquon National Wildlife Refuge holds prestigious status as a designated "Ramsar Convention on Wetlands of International Importance," which means Emiquon is a critical and essential wildlife and waterfowl habitat. Spend the day bird-watching over 264 species of birds. Dogs are permitted on leash only, unless specified hunting during waterfowl hunting season. Fishing is allowed except during migratory bird area closures; check the US Fish & Wildlife Service website and find the rules for Emiquon before heading to fish. Boating is allowed, but be sure to check the Illinois Department of Natural Resources website for fishing, hunting, and boating regulations. Emiquon is perfect for photographers, artists, and wildlife watchers, so pack your picnic lunch! Park rangers host educational and seasonal tours, so come for a tour. As truly one of the most beautiful wildlife refuges anywhere in the world, it contains over 11,122 acres of wetland habitats by the Illinois and Spoon rivers and is the largest floodplain restoration project in the Midwest.

Fulton County, Illinois, near the Illinois River, Lewistown, 309-535-2290
fws.gov/refuge/emiquon

CHECK OUT THESE OTHER NEARBY WILDLIFE GROUPS AND CULTURAL MUSEUMS

Chautauqua National Wildlife Refuge
19031 E County Rd. 2110N, Havana, 309-535-2290
fws.gov/refuge/chautauqua

Illinois State Dickson Mounds Museum
10956 N Dickson Mounds Rd., Lewistown, 309-547-3721
illinoisstatemuseum.org/content/
dickson-mounds-visitor-information

Emiquon Audubon Society
fws.gov/refuge/emiquon

WALK THROUGH HISTORY
AT SPRINGDALE CEMETERY

Springdale Cemetery & Mausoleum is a peaceful and beautiful park, offering a museum-level serving of history and one of largest cemeteries in Illinois. It was founded in 1854 and established in 1857, coming at the height of the garden- and park-like cemeteries that were popular during the Victorian era. Beautiful oak trees with twisting branches more than a century old populate these 223 acres. Walk the winding roads mixed between acres of forest, navigate greenspace, gravestones, and creeks, and cross little bridges throughout the cemetery as well as actual hiking trails and a large prairie. You can see examples of history of prominent Peorians on the tombstones and signage. You can see hawks, eagles, coyotes, and a large population of deer, as well as other local plants and trees. Prominent families who left their stamp in Peoria's history tell the stories of how Peoria became established in agriculture, industry, culture, and the distilling legacies.

Walkers, runners, and cyclists can enjoy over six miles of roads year-round. It connects to one mile of the Rock Island Trail system. Check out the 5k Run each May and Historic Cemetery Tours in October.

3014 N Prospect Rd., 309-681-1400
springdalecemetery.com

SOME NOTABLE PEOPLE BURIED AT SPRINGDALE

Octave Chanute, the father of American aviation

Famed American artist **Hedley Waycott**

Lydia Moss Bradley, founder of Bradley Polytechnic Institute, now Bradley University. Lydia was a widow and millionaire in charge of her own money a century ahead of her time. She founded businesses, was president of a bank, and was a huge philanthropist who established Laura Bradley Park.

TAKE YOUR CANINE PAL
TO BRADLEY PARK

One of Peoria's most notable people from the past is Lydia Moss Bradley, who donated 140 acres of land in memory of her daughter to create Laura Bradley Park, commonly known as Bradley Park. Lydia Moss Bradley was a woman ahead of her time, and much of Peoria's Historic West Bluff connects in many ways because of her, including the founding of Bradley University. There are three main sections of the park, with Upper Bradley Park by Main Street by Bradley University, with a nice playground and picnic area. Lower Bradley Park has baseball fields, a playground, a large pavilion, a beautiful Japanese garden, a Japanese bridge, two sand volleyball courts, tennis courts, and a frisbee golf course. A bit further back on this level are two dog parks, one for smaller dogs and one for larger dogs. There is another section by Corn Stock Theatre and Lab with another playground. The hill at Lower Bradley Park is a popular sledding site.

1317 N Park Rd., 309-682-1200
peoriaparks.org/venue/bradley-park

A FEW MORE PARKS/TRAILS TO TRY
Donovan Park
Illinois River Bluff Trail
Pimiteoui Trail Forest Park
Forest Glen
Detweiller Park
Chartwell Park
Glen Oak Park

ENGAGE IN EXCITING EVENTS
AT THE PEORIA CIVIC CENTER

The Peoria Civic Center opened in 1982 in downtown Peoria, having hosted thousands of events in its four-decade history. It has a theater, ballroom, and an exhibit hall, and is home to the Bradley University Braves men's basketball team, the Peoria Rivermen hockey team, the Peoria Symphony Orchestra, and Peoria Ballet. Events include top-name comedian shows, bands, and Broadway shows in the theater's roster. You can see demolition derbies, home shows, and conventions and events of all kinds. The Peoria Rivermen are a professional hockey team that are part of the Southern Professional Hockey League, and play at Carver Arena at the Peoria Civic Center. The Rivermen are also one of the longest continually running hockey leagues, having been founded in the 1982/83 season under the name Peoria Prancers. The Peoria Ballet performs *The Nutcracker* every December, featuring over 100 dancers and professional guest artists.

201 SW Jefferson Ave.
peoriaciviccenter.com

TIP

If you like live music and craft beer, head to Kenny's Westside Pub when you are downtown. There's great food and tons of live music weekly. 112 SW Jefferson Ave., 309-676-1693, kennyswestside.com

Peoria City Hall
Photo courtesy of Gwen Bateman

CULTURE AND HISTORY

VISIT THE HISTORIC GREENHUT MEMORIAL GAR HALL
IN DOWNTOWN PEORIA

Whiskey barons played in Peoria, and J. B. Greenhut was Peoria's version of a Rockefeller or Carnegie. Greenhut was the head of the Whiskey Trust, helping form the Great Western Distilleries, with Peoria at the center of it all. He operated one of the largest distilleries in the world. Greenhut was a Union veteran and the benefactor for the Greenhut Memorial Grand Army of the Republic (GAR) Hall, built in 1909 for Union Veterans of the Civil War, originally used for meetings and social gatherings for the members of the GAR. Built in art deco style, it features beautiful stained glass windows and original hardwood floors in the auditorium, which is filled with relics and antiques from the Civil War. A community organization, the nonprofit Central Illinois Landmarks Foundation, helped save the hall in the early 1970s, and the building has been used as a performance and event venue since. It was listed on the National Register of Historic Places in 1976.

416 Hamilton Blvd., 309-857-6844
cilfpeoria.org

PEORIA CONTINUES ITS DISTILLING HISTORY TODAY

Visit **BLACK BAND Distillery**, which is located in a historic warehouse in downtown Peoria. It is a craft distillery, producing bourbon, rye, whiskey, gin, vodka, and liqueurs with locally grown, organic grains! It is also a bar, restaurant, and shop.
1000 SW Adams St.
blackband-distillery.com

JK Williams Distilling produces high-quality whiskey with Jeff Murphy, who is a Master Distiller! JK Williams has a beautiful tasting room to enjoy a locally distilled glass of whiskey.
8635 N Industrial Rd., 617-755-5206
jkwilliamsdistilling.com

Peoria didn't just produce whiskeys; the city made beer, too! Check out **The 33 Room**, a cocktail bar dedicated to Peoria's history with Pabst Blue Ribbon.
4541 N Prospect Rd., Unit 33, Peoria Heights
the33room.com

CHECK OUT THE LONGEST-RUNNING WOMEN'S CLUB
IN THE NATION

The Peoria Women's Club was established in 1886, and is one of the longest continually running women's clubs in the country. It is a beautiful, large, brick building, built in 1893. A lot is packed inside this historic gem! It was originally a club built on the arts, but evolved into more civic, cultural, and philanthropic endeavors. Walk through the black iron rod gates into the foyer and walk across the mosaic tile, and then notice an old grandfather clock. To your right and your left you will see meeting rooms reminiscent of a Victorian home. The Peoria Women's Club is a diverse and multigenerational club, and has a social, educational, and philanthropic energy. The historic building has a beautiful, full-raked-stage music hall on the upper level original to the building. It is under a multistep fundraising and restoration plan to bring the theater/music hall back to its original grandeur.

301 NE Madison Ave., 309-370-5540
peoriawomensclub.com

TOUR THE OLDEST STANDING HOUSE
IN PEORIA, THE FLANAGAN HOUSE

The Judge John C. Flanagan House Museum was built in 1837, and holds the claim as the oldest standing home in Peoria. It was given this honor on the National Register of Historic Places in 1975. It is built in the American Federal style, and hosts a breathtaking view of the Illinois River Valley. The home was built with local limestone from the Kickapoo Creek, is decorated with period pieces, including a beautiful collection of antiques. The Flanagan House is owned by the Peoria Historical Society, which offers tours. The home is available for rentals, and is the headquarters for the Peoria Chapter of the Daughters of the American Revolution. There are beautiful floral gardens in both the front and back. Tours are open the first and third Sunday of the month from 1 to 4 p.m. and by appointment.

942 NE Glen Oak Ave., 309-674-1921
peoriahistoricalsociety.com/houses

TIP

The Peoria Historical Society is a nonprofit organization whose mission is to preserve and celebrate Peoria's history. It offers educational and entertaining programs for local and out-of-town visitors. It also collaborates with other preservation organizations, and is a partner with the Peoria Riverfront Museum to display local artifacts and share history in the museum. 309-674-1921, peoriahistoricalsociety.com

RIDE THE GLASS ELEVATOR
AT TOWER PARK IN PEORIA HEIGHTS

One of the best views of the Illinois River Valley is at the top of the water tower at Tower Park, once you ride the glass elevator up. It is open seasonally from April through October, and there are three observation decks with telescopes to see the glorious views, which are nearly 20 miles on clear days. It's the only one of its kind in the nation. The tower is 200 feet high, is a maroon red color, a gigantic woodpecker on the middle side of the tower. Bring the family and pack a sack lunch, and play on the playground below. Numerous community events are hosted at Tower Park, such as Second Fridays, with artists, vendors, fire spinners, food trucks, and even a drum circle with the Peoria Drum Circle; and live concerts the first Fridays of the month from May through October, offering food and a mobile bar for the grownups!

1222 E Kingman Ave., Peoria Heights, 309-686-2385
peoriaheights.org/tower-park

TIP
While in Peoria Heights, have a cocktail on a rooftop at The Twelve Bar Lounge. 4500 N Prospect Rd., Peoria Heights

SHOP
AT THE MOSS AVENUE
ANTIQUE SALE & FESTIVAL

Savoring the days of yesteryear, hundreds of people can be seen strolling along the Moss Avenue festival each year, enjoying the sights, smells, and sounds of over 40 years of tradition. The event grows bigger and better each year. Historic Moss Avenue truly shines with Peoria's historic architectural homes with the bluff side hosting incredible yards, mature trees, and hidden treasures of details all around. The annual Moss Avenue Antique Sale & Festival takes place on a Saturday in June each year, from the 1100 to 1800 blocks of Moss. You can bring the entire family. and stay all day, finding treasures among the antiques, vintage and repurposed items, crafters, antique sellers, vendors, food and drink purveyors, and live music and entertainers. There are trinkets and treasures galore! There is lots of local art to purchase. It truly is a wonderful, blocks-long, flea market festival.

309-648-2538
facebook.com/mossavenueantiquesalefestival/?fref=ts

TIP

Market on Moss at StoneWell Gardens is a French market that takes place in a 100-year-old Victorian farmhouse surrounded with beautiful gardens inspired by Beatrix Potter's *Peter Rabbit* children's stories. 2320 W Moss Ave., West Peoria, stonewellgardens.blogspot.com

VISIT THE PETTENGILL-MORRON HOUSE MUSEUM
ON MOSS AVENUE

Lucy and Moses Pettengill were staunch abolitionists and conductors along the Underground Railroad, helping slaves escape to freedom. Moses Pettengill was a wealthy Peoria businessman. Lucy passed away in 1864. Moses later remarried and lived in the home upon its completion in 1868 on Moss Avenue. It is now owned by the Peoria Historical Society (PHS) and is one of two historic house museums. It is built in the Second Empire architectural style, with some additions. Each holiday season PHS hosts its Holiday Home Tour of both house museums, with the houses decorated with different historic Christmas themes each year, and volunteers dressed for the time period as well. Past years' themes have included a Victorian Christmas and Charles Dickens's Christmas. Both homes are beautifully decorated and get you in the mood to celebrate the holidays. Tours of the Pettengill-Morron House Museum are scheduled each Thursday from 10 a.m. to 2 p.m. and by appointment.

1212 W Moss Ave., 309-674-1921
peoriahistoricalsociety.com/houses

INTERESTED IN ILLINOIS HISTORY WITH THE CIVIL WAR AND UNDERGROUND RAILROAD?

Visit the **Owen Lovejoy House Museum** in Princeton, Illinois, about 45 minutes north of Peoria. It was built in 1838 by Illinois congressman and staunch abolitionist Owen Lovejoy. As a conductor on the Underground Railroad, he hid runaway slaves inside his home. Much history is packed throughout the home, and a glimpse of the tiny compartment where the escaped slaves would hide brings the era to life. Lovejoy was vociferous about his anti-slavery views and gave assistance to many souls who escaped north to freedom. It is listed as a National Historic Landmark and is open seasonally.

905 E Peru St., Princeton, 815-879-9151
owenlovejoyhomestead.com

A little side trip while in Princeton, Illinois, is to visit the historic **Red Covered Bridge** or the **Captain Swift Bridge** after you visit the Owen Lovejoy House Museum.

Visit the **Abraham Lincoln Memorial Garden**, the **Abraham Lincoln House, Abraham Lincoln Memorial Museum**, and **Lincoln's New Salem**, all a little over an hour away from Peoria.

SAVOR SCRUMPTIOUS FALL COLORS
ON THE WORLD'S MOST BEAUTIFUL DRIVE, GRAND VIEW DRIVE

Local legend has it that President Teddy Roosevelt visited the drive in 1910, and called it the world's most beautiful drive. Whether legendary or not, Grand View Drive a definite for anyone visiting from out of town at any time of year. It is listed on the National Register of Historic Places and was created in 1903. Grand View Drive is two and a half miles long, with dozens of historic and extraordinary homes. There is a walking trail and benches to gaze from. Autumn is especially beautiful with the fall colors: burgundy, burnt orange, golden yellow, and oak brown creating a panoramic landscape each year. Along the drive you will notice Becker Park with some hoops, baseball fields, picnic tables, and a playground courtesy of the Peoria Park District. Pets are welcome, as are inline skaters, and skateboard areas are available.

3210 Grand View Dr., 309-682-6684
peoriaparks.org/grand-view-drive

BRING YOUR BIKE
TO RIDE BICYCLE SAFETY TOWN

Bicycle Safety Town came to be in the mid-1960s, and joined the Peoria Park District in the mid-1970s to teach bicycle safety rules of the road/town. It is charming, with little roads and traffic signals. Kids will have a blast learning while they ride over the overpass and ramps, and obey 70 traffic signs. The bicycle track is almost three acres and has almost 4,000 feet of little roads, one-way streets, and curves. The park is open every day and is free to use, except when educational courses are taking place, so be sure to check the website. You can spend the day: Bring a picnic lunch to eat; there is a playground for toddlers while the bigger kids ride the bikes on the track, and a water fountain, too. It's close to the Rock Island Greenway section of the Rock Island Trail system.

6518 N Sheridan Rd., 309-682-6684
peoriaparks.org/facilities/bicycle-safety-town

JOURNEY
TO HISTORIC PEORIA CITY HALL

Built in 1899, historic Peoria City Hall sits next to the Peoria Civic Center. Listed on the National Register of Historic Places, the building is a giant piece of art outside, inside, and top to bottom. It's visually striking with red sandstone, and built in the German Renaissance architectural style. Walk into the entryway, and you will approach a beautiful white marble statue first shown at the 1893 Chicago World's Fair. Everything inside is gorgeous: From the floors to the on the walls. The ornate black metal on the staircase runs from the first floor to the top of the building, with a view to the top from the bottom, and a large dome at the top center. The City Council Chamber has an elaborate mural on the back wall by an artist known as Peaco, commissioned in 1912, and depicts three feminine muses highlighting themes of community, industry, and peace.

419 Fulton St., 309-494-2273
peoriagov.org

PERFECT POTTERY AND PAINTING WITH THE LITTLES
AT FIRED UP POTTERY

Visitors to Peoria seeing family and friends would enjoy an artful morning or afternoon at Fired Up Pottery, picking out the perfect item to paint. It's affordable, too. There is a nominal studio fee for adults and even less for kids under 18, with pottery pieces in a range of prices. A typical creative session will take one to three hours on average, and you are allowed to bring snacks and drinks into the studio, so pack a lunch for the littles. Adults over age 21 are allowed to bring in wine or beer! Make sure to remember that the pottery has a drying period, so you will receive a text reminder in about one week to pick up your pottery. Pieces to pick include plates, mugs, bowls, serving pieces, banks, boxes, animal figurines, and seasonal items. The paint and glazes are safe for kids and are lead-free. Reservations are recommended.

4532 N Prospect Rd., Peoria Heights, 309-685-8906
firedupstudios.biz

TIP

Wheel Art is another studio to create pottery on the wheel, and a school to teach people of all levels how to make and paint pottery. 1101 SW Washington St., 309-306-1741, sites.google.com/site/wheelartpotterystudio

---

REENVISION TOMORROW
WITH ART INC

Located inside the Romain Arts & Culture Center, a nonprofit group, Artists ReEnvisioning Tomorrow (ART Inc) brings all walks of life together with art and education, and through culture! Located in the heart of Peoria's downtown, in a former school building, Nikki and Jonathon Romain formed a nonprofit to help serve children with arts and education, no matter whether they could pay. They believed in a vision to make art available to everybody in Peoria, including the underserved parts of the community. There are art camps for kids during spring break, Paint with Jonathon art classes, and an after-school arts and leadership academy for kids, EmpowHer Our Girls. There's also theatrical productions, dance classes, cultural events like the De Los Muertos: Love Never Dies Event, and film classes for teens. Affordable rentals are also available.

919 NE Jefferson Ave., 309-713-3744
artincpeoria.org

GET CREATIVE
AT ART AT THE BODEGA

People of all skill levels can have fun, learn, and get in touch with their creative side at Art at the Bodega. You can walk in for some amazing canvas painting, no skill level required, just bring your imagination. They have fun days to come in and paint your own fabulous wood sign for your home. They offer do-it-yourself projects in canvas, pottery, mosaics, and clay, as well as farmhouse signs and to-go kits.

You can even get subscription boxes shipped to your home. Have fun molding wet clay in your hands and the Just Try It Wheel Throwing Class! They offer summer art camps for kids, adult paint classes, and many paint and art classes for the kiddos. There are snacks and sodas to buy for the kids, and some wine and beer for those over age 21.

309-431-1307
theartbodega.com

JOIN PEORIA OUTDOOR ADVENTURE/ BIG PICTURE PEORIA
FOR A MURAL TOUR

The Fall Mural Bike Ride around Peoria offers two options for this spectacular scenic tour: 8 a.m. start from Bushwhacker for a 21-mile, looped ride and 9 a.m. start from the Peoria Riverfront Museum for a seven-mile, looped ride.

Highlighting over 60 art murals, traveling along several miles, you get a taste of the energy and artistry here in Peoria with a well-rounded art experience. From jazz to diversity, inclusion to love, greetings from Peoria to true masterpieces, you get to immerse yourself in the journey and learn so much about this fair city. One notable on the Peoria County Courthouse is *Abraham Blue* by Doug Leunig in 2018, which expresses the seriousness of Abraham Lincoln's life, and his experience in Peoria. Peoria Outdoor Adventure hosts and shares sports and recreation events in the Peoria area, and promotes anything outdoorsy, eateries, and the wonderful people in Peoria.

peoriaoutdooradventure.com

GET
THE BIG PICTURE PEORIA

Come see the Big Picture in Peoria for arts and entertainment. Big Picture Peoria is a nonprofit group established by community volunteers to help provide arts and art opportunities to all people living in the Peoria area. Big Picture collaborates art with education, art mentoring, and art classes, and provides these free to the community. They host a free street festival that brings together local musicians and artists in the trendy Warehouse District, which has food and numerous artisans showing how they make their crafts in live presentations, a flash mob, and lots of kids' activities. Big Picture believes that public art helps ensure a happy and healthy community. Another project they did was the giant *Abraham Blue* mural on the outside of the Peoria County Courthouse in 2018. Big Picture partners with other local nonprofits, government agencies, and businesses to help provide a healthy art community in Peoria.

bigpicturepeoria.org

TIP

Visit the Richard Pryor sculpture, located on the corner of Washington and State Streets, created by the famous artist Preston Jackson. Richard Pryor was born and raised in Peoria and was an internationally famous comedian and actor. The sculpture, dedicated in 2015, was a project of the African American Hall of Fame Museum and the Richard Pryor Sculpture Project Committee.

IMMERSE YOURSELF IN ART
WITH THE PEORIA ART GUILD

The Peoria Art Guild was established over 140 years ago, and their theme is "bringing art to the community, and the community to art." They host numerous events such as the Peoria Fine Art Fair each year, and it's one of the biggest art events in Central Illinois, showcasing over 130 artists locally, nationally, and from around the world. It brings in visitors from all over the country, and can brag about drawing 8,000 to 10,000 visitors to what is one of the oldest fine arts fairs in America. You can bring the entire family and view the amazing art, live music, food, and tons of activities for all ages. They also host the Sculpture Walk Peoria Outdoor Exhibit. Leaders in the arts and leaders in the community chose sculptures from artists from around the country. There will be eight featured sculptures along both sides of Washington Street, from the Peoria Riverfront Museum to the Bob Michel Bridge.

203 Harrison St., 309-637-2787
peoriaartguild.org

OTHER ART FESTIVALS
India Fest
Peoria Art Guild Fine Art Fair

CELEBRATE HISPANIC CULTURE
AT FIESTA EN EL RIO

Peoria's Hispanic population is booming, bringing numerous amazing businesses, people, and Hispanic culture to the Peoria area. For over 14 years, Peoria has celebrated the Fiesta en el Rio Event that highlights and celebrates Hispanic culture. There are children's activities such as a petting zoo, face painting, and even bouncy houses, as well as informational and vendor booths. Learn how to dance the salsa or mamba, and enjoy live Mexican music being played. It truly is a fiesta: Enjoy delicious food as well! Through the event, the Greater Peoria Hispanic Chamber of Commerce wants the entire community of Peoria to come together to experience the wonderful things the Hispanic culture has to offer. The Fiesta en el Rio takes place once a year on the Peoria RiverFront Events/CEFCU Center Stage @ The Landing.

FEEL THE HEAT
AT J DRAPER GLASS LLC

The art scene is hot, quite literally, at J Draper Glass LLC—hot, liquid glass, that is. For a truly unique experience, venture out on a First Friday event to see the artists dip and spin and swirl the brightly colored liquid glass and shape it. Hot glass is simply beautiful, and the anticipation during the wait for it to cool and harden is incredible. J Draper Glass also provides hands-on hot glass opportunities for patrons, and they request calling ahead for an appointment. Owner and instructor Jeremie Draper studied extensively and has a bachelor of fine arts degree from Southern Illinois University. Some of her inspirations honor the Italian color styles, and she is passionate about her art form. Her studio is located at the Studios On Sheridan at the Sunbeam Building, at the Peoria International Airport Gift Shop, Exhibit A Gallery, and at the Peoria Riverfront Museum.

734 W Main St., 309-339-6244
jdraperglass.com

HERE COMES THE SUN: THE SUN FOUNDATION, WHERE ART, NATURE, AND SCIENCE MEET!

The Sun Foundation was formed in the 1960s, and is a nonprofit organization that helps teach both children and adults about art, nature, and science. One of its most popular events is Art & Science in the Woods, which teaches people ages six to adult in a five-day-long camp. The camp unites students with professional artists and scientists to learn about art, science, and survival skills, all outdoors in nature. Through education, they help teach others how to live in harmony with nature. The Peoria Clean Water Celebration is the largest of its kind in the world. It teaches how to protect our water and takes place each year in the spring at the Peoria Civic Center. Enjoy seeing the worms, fish, clams, and tadpoles while enjoying an assortment of programs that educate in a fun and impactful way. You will learn all about ecosystems, water, plants, and animals, in storytelling form, demonstrations, and interactive activities.

1276 Sun Rd., Washburn, 309-246-8403
sunfoundation.org

Lily Scalf
Photo courtesy of Jerri Frances

SHOPPING
AND FASHION

SCORE ANTIQUES AND FUN
AT LITTLE SHOP OF HOARDERS

Bowling alley seats in brilliant light blue, bowling alley scoreboards, and some of the very best antique and flea market shopping around can be found at Little Shop of Hoarders. Located on historic downtown Second Street in Chillicothe, the store, unlike its fun name, is well-organized and filled with books, antiques, knickknacks, furniture, and more. The proprietors host a complimentary coffee and cookie bar, and encourage guests to sit and chitchat for a while. There is no rush; meander at your own pace to find the perfect treasure for your home. Find a fireplace mantel, a writer's desk, or an antique dining room table and chairs. Items are reasonably priced, and are priced to sell, too! Looking for a special piece to use as a hutch, or want to find something to refinish? This is your place.

941 N 2nd St., Chillicothe, 309-657-2505
littleshopofhoardersil.com

LOVE ANTIQUES AND FLEA MARKETS?
Looking 4 Treasures
Primitiques
Anne's Anteex
The Attic
The Pickers Daughter
Two Sisters and a Warehouse
Callahan Antiques

ENJOY PRECIOUS FLOWERS
FROM STEMS BY ALLISON

Stems by Allison is a super-chic boutique and floral shop. A WEEK 25 News Viewer's Choice Award Winner in 2021, Allison Carmack deserves all the accolades for sharing her gifts with all of us. Floral designing runs in her blood, and she and her family have been in the flower business for close to four decades. Allison developed a style that you could describe as gorgeous and eclectic, giving designs her unique stamp. You can order flowers for a large wedding, sympathy arrangements for funerals, and corsages for proms. Whatever the event, she can pull something beautiful together for you with custom orders. Her shop is more than floral design: You can buy cool, unique decorative signs, plants, clothing, candles, and too many other items to list. There are a few vendors inside, and the place smells delectable every time you walk in. You can purchase grab-and-go arrangements on special days of the year, such as poinsettias for Christmas and bouquets of fresh flowers for Valentine's Day and Mother's Day.

915 Second St., Chillicothe, 309-258-8596
stemsbyallison.com

MORE BOUTIQUES

Cranberry Creek	Picket Fence	Sweet Finds
Cool Thingz	Waxwing Books	Chillicothe Town Theater
Starfish Cottage	Covered Wagon	Little Land
		of Candy N' More

CATCH
REPURPOSING IN STYLE
AT KELLER STATION

Meshing Peoria's history with the railroads, Keller Station was once a stop along the Rock Island and Peoria Railway and is now used as a multipurpose shopping, dining, and business center under the direction of brilliant building developer Katie Kim, who has a knack for taking an old building and repurposing it, giving it a new second life. This transformation has been nothing short of visionary in its scope. The station hosts Drive-In Movie Theatre nights during the summer months, which are always sold out! There are weekly Keller Station Farmers Markets on Wednesdays. There is a popular coffee shop called [CxT] Roasting Company, and tons of specialty shops and businesses as well. The list of businesses filling in the station is growing quickly, so be sure to check out their website when visiting Peoria to get up-to-date information. Bring the entire family to The Noshery—six different restaurants and one place to eat!

6035 N Knoxville Ave., 309-693-9900
kellerstation.com

DIAMONDS ARE A GIRL'S BEST FRIEND
AT JONES BROTHERS JEWELERS

Jones Brothers Jewelers was established in 1939 and is now owned by the dynamic duo of Bob and Mia Woolsey. They sell wedding and engagement rings, loose diamonds, and elegant watches, earrings, necklaces, and more. No matter the budget, everyone can find something at different price points, and will be treated with respect and kindness. When you walk in you will notice the difference about this store immediately. You will be greeted with a warm smile, and notice that the energy in the store is fabulous, and you will feel like you are chatting with an old family friend, with no pressure at all. They offer jewelry repair with a master goldsmith and top-of-the-line repair equipment to bring the jewelry back to life. Want a custom design? Bring your heirloom jewelry in and work with the jewelers to design it how you want.

7705 N Grand Prairie Dr., 309-692-3228
jonesbros.com

OTHER JEWELRY STORES
Bremer Jewelry
Potter & Anderson Jewelry & Fine Gifts
Carlson's Custom Jewelry
Roger G. Burke Jewelers
Kevin Kelly Jewelry

VISIT THE NARNIA WARDROBE
AT THE BOOK RACK GIFT BOOKTIQUE

One of the most amazing independent book stores in Peoria, the Book Rack Gift Booktique has thousands of books for you to purchase, and has drawn customers from around the country to visit the Narnia Wardrobe located there. The shop was featured in an article in *Forbes* magazine on the store's Bedtime Stories with Book Rack Program, which prompted a writer from Tripadvisor to visit and pen her own article on the store and the Narnia Wardrobe. The Narnia Wardrobe is the entryway to the children's picture book room and provides a wonderful experience for children (adults are welcome, too) as they walk through the wardrobe into another room with books. The back wall has the Narnia forest on it, and the lamppost sports a real lamppost top and flaming bulb. Don't forget to check out the monthly, literary-themed Candle and Melt Pouring Workshops.

4408 N Knoxville Ave., 309-370-7683

TWO MORE BOOKSTORES
I Know You Like A Book
Lit. on Fire Books

IT'S A MARVELOUS NIGHT FOR A MOON DANCE
AT THE MOON DANCER BOUTIQUE

One of Peoria's favorite and most eclectic boutiques offers more than just a shopping experience, located in the heart of Peoria at the Studios On Sheridan in the Sunbeam Building. The owner, affectionately known as Miss Moon, Julie Vonachen, serves the store and the community with a spirit of love. Shopping at the Moon Dancer is an experience and a destination for people looking for the greater meanings in life. It sells to a diverse customer base, with some holistic items and Bohemian clothing that is unique and not trendy. Its mission is to sell "fair trade labeled merchandise," meaning it was not made in a sweatshop, and the people who made the clothing were paid a fair wage. New customers always comment on how good the store smells! They sell incense, candles, oils, homemade soaps, and lotions, as well as jewelry made by local artisans. They also host health and wellness classes.

933 N Sheridan Rd., 309-676-6160

TIP
If you love Moon Dancer, you will also love Relics, a specialty gift shop with unique items for house decor, books, plants, and jewelry. You can find tons of locally made arts and crafts, and Peoria stickers, postcards, and other Peoria trinkets. 3827 N Sheridan Rd., 309-681-9588

SAVOR MID-CENTURY MODERN, ART DECO, AND VINTAGE NOSTALGIA
AT URBAN ARTIFACTS

Located in the former Sunbeam Bakery, Urban Artifacts sells vintage and antique goods, specializing in items from the 1930s through 1980s, but not limited to that. Walk inside and nostalgia simply oozes all over the place, taking you back in time. They have a display of local history authored by local artists, and a rack of T-shirts is dedicated to past favorite stores, restaurants, and bars in Peoria that have long been closed. There is a section of plastic and metal lunch boxes with Care Bears, Strawberry Shortcake, G.I. Joe, and any type of favorite childhood character one could think of. There is a fabulous collection of vintage toys and a nice cabinet filled with old John Deere and Caterpillar tractor toys. There are huge, brightly colored, neon and metal advertising signs for sale. Find an antique jukebox, coin-operated games, and machines, vintage and mid-century modern gadgets, magazines, and other memorabilia. It's the flea market lover's paradise.

925 N Sheridan Rd., 309-361-7430
urbanartifactspeoria.com

HAVE ENVIRONMENTALLY RESPONSIBLE FUN
AT WHISKEY CITY SALVAGE

Located in the trendy Warehouse District, Whiskey City Salvage helps save historic treasures from Peoria to be reused anywhere! They have a nice variety of vintage pieces that were customized and repurposed for today. Whiskey City Salvage rescued some old bowling alley flooring from a classic Peoria bowling alley that was demolished, and added it to the front panel of a Peoria bar. Find your perfect table, and have it custom-cut so it works best for your family. Bring in that old, oversized barn door and have them turn it into a one-of-a-kind kitchen island. Peek at the photos on their Facebook page, and you will see a round tabletop added to an elegant old baptismal font base to use as a dining room table or in the man-cave or she-shed. They specialize in rehabbing and reusing resources!

1000 SW Jefferson St., 309-643-1692

TIP
Don't Miss Peoria Architectural Salvage LLC. 2000 SW Adams St., 309-643-4593, peoriasalvage.com

SWEETEN YOUR DAY
AT PINK SUGAR BOUTIQUE

Pink Sugar Boutique is a trendy women's clothing store located in the popular Junction City Shopping Center, which houses locally owned, high-end retail boutiques. Pink Sugar is the place to go to shop for exclusive brands and classic designer fashion for your wardrobe. The owners have exquisite taste, pride themselves on warm and welcoming customer service, and offer a wide variety of clothing to choose from, from companies from all over the country. Pink Sugar offers everything from day-to-day wear, to the perfect dress or jacket to stand out at that extra-special event! The styles that you can find are higher-end brands that range from denim to leather. Drink a mimosa and shop at their Spring Sip & Shop Event. You can also count on help from the owners/stylists to help you match your new outfit with just the right locally designed jewelry and accessories.

5805 N Humboldt Ave., Ste. 2, 309-713-1637
thinkpinksugar.com

PEORIA LOVES ITS BOUTIQUES!

Apricot Lane Boutique
5901 N Prospect Rd., Ste. 4
309-691-2230

Blue Boutique
7424 N Orange Prairie Rd.
309-693-1300

Belle Mie
5901 N Prospect Rd., Ste. 12
309-693-7777

Random Boutique
5901 N Prospect Rd., Ste. 18
309-689-0995

Juli's Glamour Boutique
819 NE Monroe St.

Normandy's Boutique
2200 W War Memorial Dr.
309-981-0346
normandysboutique.com

A Perfect Pear Boutique
4544 N Prospect Rd. A
Peoria Heights, 309-688-7327
aperfectpearboutique.com

Janet's Just For You
1750 N Sheridan Rd., 309-685-7844

Bello Couture Boutique
4450 N Prospect Rd., Ste. C5
Peoria Heights, 309-839-8988

Curvology
4703 N University St., 309-643-1472
mycurvology.com

Coral Ray Boutique
1010 S Western Ave., 630-634-5191

So Chic Boutique
4605 N Prospect Rd.
Peoria Heights, 309-670-0465
thesochicboutique.com

Moxie's Resale
929 N Sheridan Rd., 309-423-2109

**Wishing Star Boutique
by Tabatha, Inc.**
104 Walnut St., Washington
309-839-8046
facebook.com/
wishingstarboutiquebytabatha/
?tn-str=k*f

SPEND MAY THROUGH SEPTEMBER
AT THE PEORIA RIVERFRONT FARMERS MARKET

The Peoria Riverfront Market runs on Saturdays from 8 a.m. to noon from the middle of May through September, located directly across the street from the Peoria Riverfront Museum. You will find the freshest of the fresh veggies and fruits from locally grown farms and gardens. Vendors will have eggs, berries, cheese, and breads for you to cook healthier, while supporting local farms and gardens. Local artisans sell homemade pottery, jewelry, candles, and soaps, too. Sometimes there will be fresh omelets and live music, and it seems more like a festival than a simple farmers market. Don't forget to purchase local honey! Purchase local meats from local farms, and baked goods from right here in Central Illinois. The market takes place in the 200 block of Water Street, by a large, free parking lot. Enjoy the fresh air, community spirit, and lovely views of the Illinois River.

212 SW Water St., 309-671-5555
visitdowntownpeoria.com/peoria-riverfront-market

CHECK OUT THESE OTHER FARMERS MARKETS

Peoria Farmers Market at Metro Centre   Morton Farmers Market
Keller Station Farmers Market   Junction City Farmers Market

ACTIVITIES
BY SEASON

SPRING

Enjoy Precious Flowers from Stems by Allison, 127

Spend May through September at the Peoria Riverfront Farmers Market, 136

Find Beautiful Hidden Gems in Sommer Farm Park, Part of the Peoria Park District, 87

Run, Walk, and Cycle on the Rock Island Trail, 59

Populate Dozer Park with the Peoria Chiefs, 76

SUMMER

Celebrate Peoria's Juneteenth Fest at John Gwynn Park, 64

A City within a City: Scampers Unite at the Summer Camp Music Festival, 40

Get Creative at Art at the Bodega, 117

Walk through Thousands of Giant Sunflowers at Jubilee State Park and Stay to Play, 68

Eat a Hot Dog at Lou's Drive-In, 30

Take a 16.4 Mile HLC River Jaunt along the Illinois River, Hosted by the Chillicothe Chamber of Commerce, 80

Canoe, Fish, or Birdwatch at the Banner Marsh State Fish and Wildlife Area, 94

Shop at the Moss Avenue Antique Sale & Festival, 109

Join Peoria Outdoor Adventure/Big Picture Peoria for a Mural Tour, 118

Hear the Heritage Ensemble, 65

Join Us in July for the Heart of Illinois Fair, 55

• •

FALL

WINTER

SUGGESTED
ITINERARIES

CLASSIC PEORIA AREA DAYDREAM

Find Family Fun at the Peoria Riverfront Museum, 73

Visit Wildlife Prairie Park, Jewel of the Midwest, 77

Take the Beefeater Challenge at Peoria's Alexander's Steakhouse!, 8

SPORT ENTHUSIASTS

Populate Dozer Park with the Peoria Chiefs, 76

Take Your Canine Pal to Bradley Park, 100

Have a Paintball Battle at Chillicothe Paintball Pits, 82

Run the Steamboat Peoria and Race through Historic Parts of the City, 79

Bring Your Bike to Ride Bicycle Safety Town, 113

Motorcyclists Unite in the Peoria Motorcycle Club, 84

SEEKING FUN AND MUSIC

A City within a City: Scampers Unite at the Summer Camp Music Festival, 40

Come See a Show at the Peoria Players Theatre, 49

Celebrate Irish Culture at the Peoria Irish Fest, 62

Party like a Rock Star at Crusens Bar, 70

Willkommen to Peoria Oktoberfest, 63

Do a Stand-Up Comedy Routine at the Jukebox Comedy Club, 56

Engage in Exciting Events at the Peoria Civic Center, 101

• •

GOING ON A DATE

A Bottle of Red, a Bottle of White, Beckon at Paparazzi Restaurant, 14

Dine near a 30-Foot-Tall, Indoor Waterfall at Connected Restaurant, 22

Ride the Glass Elevator at Tower Park in Peoria Heights, 108

Relax at the Mackinaw Valley Winery and Vineyard, 48

Celebrate the Woodlands at Forest Park Nature Center, 88

See Peoria's Outdoor Theater under the Tent at the Corn Stock Theatre, 50

Enjoy Upscale Dining at Jonah's Seafood House, 12

FOR US FOODIES

Celebrate Blissful Delish at Trefzger's Bakery, 13

Cool Off at Yeni's Palarte Ice Cream Shop, 25

Meet the Patron Saint of Cheesecake Baking at Triple Dipple's, 4

Eat a Hot Dog at Lou's Drive-In, 30

Go Around the World with Midwestern Hospitality at One World Cafe, 6

Try Authentic Lebanese Mediterranean Food at Restaurant Kabab-G's, 26

Welcome to Water Street at Kelleher's Irish Pub & Eatery, 18

Stir Up Tacos, Tequila, and Punch at Cayenne Restaurant, 28

Explore a Historic Location at the Blue Duck Barbecue Tavern, 35

Don't Be a Jerk, Eat Authentic Caribbean Cuisine
    at the Jerk Hut Restaurant!, 20

PLAYFUL FUN WITH KIDS

Go on Safari at the Wild Kingdom at Peoria Zoo, 47

Keep the Big Wheels Turning at Wheels O' Time Museum, 86

Lace Your Skates Year-Round at Owens Center, 57

Follow the Yellow Brick Road at the Illinois Oz Fest, 91

• •

FUN IN THE SUN OUTDOORS

PEORIA FUN TIMES

• •

HIDDEN TREASURES

Tour the Oldest Standing House in Peoria, the Flanagan House, 107

Wet Your Whistle in a Really Nice Dive Bar in a Garage at Mike's Tavern, 36

Pick Your Apples Right off the Trees at Tanners Orchard, 58

Celebrate the Woodlands at Forest Park Nature Center, 88

Attend the Chrysanthemum Show at Luthy Botanical Garden, 66

Walk through History at Springdale Cemetery, 98

Visit the Historic Greenhut Memorial GAR Hall in Downtown Peoria, 104

Sweeten Your Day at Pink Sugar Boutique, 134

● ●

INDEX

● ●